Puffin Books
Editor: Kaye Web

The Puffin Book of

The magic in this book will not enable you to
turn your schoolteacher into a chocolate-cream
frog, or cause a mighty palace to arise in the
back garden. But it does show you how to
perform exciting, amusing, mysterious and
somewhat joyous conjuring tricks, to entertain
your friends and cause them to think you no end
of a clever chap (or girl, of course). It also
shows you how to have a bit of fun making
some of the things used in the tricks, without
also making too much mess.

Norman Hunter, who conjured up the Professor
Branestawm stories for you, has included several
tricks that he performs in his own Chinese magic
act, which he lets off under the name of Ho Wat
Fun.

Jill McDonald has waved her magic pen and
produced out of her newest hat the delicious
illustrations.

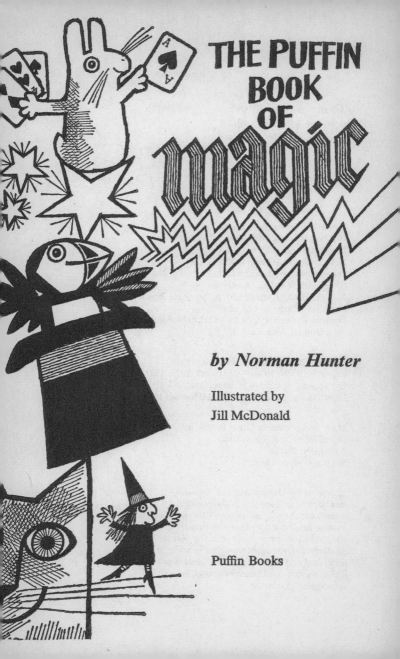

THE PUFFIN
BOOK
OF
magic

*by **Norman Hunter***

Illustrated by
Jill McDonald

Puffin Books

To my grandchildren,
who are kind enough to
like my magic

Puffin Books, Penguin Books Ltd,
Harmondsworth, Middlesex, England
Penguin Books, 625 Madison Avenue,
New York, New York 10022, U.S.A.
Penguin Books Australia Ltd,
Ringwood, Victoria, Australia
Penguin Books Canada Ltd, 41 Steelcase Road West,
Markham, Ontario, Canada
Penguin Books (N.Z.) Ltd, 182–190 Wairau Road,
Auckland 10, New Zealand

First published 1968
Reprinted 1969, 1970, 1971 (twice), 1973, 1975, 1976 (twice)
Copyright © Norman Hunter, 1968
Illustrations copyright © Jill McDonald, 1968

Made and printed in Great Britain by
Hazell Watson & Viney Ltd,
Aylesbury, Bucks
Set in Linotype Times

Contents

I hope you notice that I haven't called this *The Puffin Book of Easy Magic*. There are a lot of books on a lot of subjects that say, in effect, anybody can do anything; everything is easy. But the truth is that nobody can do anything much unless he learns how to, and nothing worth doing is easy.

Doing magic properly isn't all that easy. You've got to learn how to do a trick, and practise doing it, before you can hope to make a success of showing it to an audience. But although it isn't so very easy, neither is it very difficult. Think of reciting Baa Baa Blacksheep. Easy enough. Ah, but you've jolly well got to learn the words or you can't do it. It's the same with magic. The magic I have explained in this book isn't difficult. But it isn't so easy that you can go charging off to do the tricks to an audience without having practised them.

Do I disappoint you? Do you want to chuck this book out of the window? Well do make sure the window is open first.

The reason why you have to practise a conjuring trick, even an easy conjuring trick, before you show it to an audience is that you are doing secret things which the audience must not suspect. You not only have to do these secret things as if you weren't doing them, you also have to entertain the audience with some amusing remarks – conjurers call this 'patter' – at the same time.

You must learn to do the secret things without looking as if you were doing anything unusual. But this isn't really very difficult. People sometimes do it at school, I believe, pretending to be doing their lessons while they're really doing something else. Frightfully wrong of course and naturally Puffin readers never do that (let's hope).

You must also learn the words you are going to say. But don't learn them off by heart and speak them as if you were reciting a lesson. Learn what you are going to say but don't feel you must use exactly the same words every time. In fact, learn the kind of things you're going to say rather than the actual words. Then you'll be able to say them more naturally.

You must also practise the ordinary things you are going to do, to make sure you can do them neatly.

It's surprising how easy it is to make a mess of doing something quite ordinary when you try to do it in front of an audience. Suppose you are going to light a candle. Easy enough, you say. But this is the kind of thing that can happen if you try to light a candle in front of an audience without practising first:

You open the box of matches, but the drawer part is upside down and all the matches fall out. You put them back and strike a match. But you strike too hard and the match breaks. You strike another one and it goes out before you can light the candle. You try again and get the candle alight. Then you blow out the match and blow the candle out too, by mistake.

Of course all this would be very funny if you did it on purpose, as a funny act. But if you wanted to make sure of doing all those things wrong you'd have to practise doing them wrong. Fancy having to practise just as much to do a thing wrong as to do it right. But there it is. So do practise your tricks before you do a show to an audience. You'll be glad you did.

Now a word about the way you do the tricks. I don't mean the way you handle the articles you use or the way you make the secret moves, I mean the attitude you adopt.

A lot of conjurers, even professional conjurers, make the

mistake of doing their tricks in a way that suggests to the audience that they are cheating them in some way. They present their tricks as a sort of challenge to the audience to find out how they are done.

Never, never do this. There is always likely to be someone in an audience who will think he knows how a trick is done and want to let the audience know how clever he is. If you do the tricks in a way that seems to say, 'See if you can spot this one,' or, 'Now I'm going to fool you,' this kind of person will be on you like a shot and you'll have no end of trouble.

What you have to do is to present your tricks simply as an entertainment. You must try to make the audience accept your show and enjoy it just as they would any other kind of entertainment. Never suggest that they should try to guess how the tricks are done.

Of course it is quite likely that some smart chap in the audience may call out, 'I know how that's done,' or, 'It went up your sleeve.' So how do you deal with a situation like that? I'll tell you.

You make a joke of it. If someone says, 'I know how that's done,' you reply, 'Well, there's nothing in that, so do I.'

If someone says, 'It went up your sleeve,' you say, 'Of course it did, why do you suppose conjurers have sleeves?' If someone says, 'Seen it on the Telly,' as someone may, you counter it with, 'Aren't you lucky. You've seen it on the Telly and now you're going to see it live.'

You see the idea. Never take up a challenge. Never be upset or cross at remarks from the audience. Make a joke about them. You'll have the rest of the audience on your side anyway because nobody likes people who try to spoil a show. And by making the sort of remarks I have suggested, you make the clever chap feel it wasn't really worth while calling out because he hasn't succeeded in making himself look clever after all.

If you follow this advice, there is no reason why you shouldn't become, not merely a good magician, but a very good magician. You will enjoy your performances more, and so will your audiences.

N.H.

TRICKS WITH ORDINARY THINGS

OH DEAR HER MOTHER WILL BE CROSS

Cutting a girl in two

This isn't quite as sensational as sawing through a woman but it's a very surprising piece of magic and not difficult to do.

You have a long piece of rope which you wind round the waist of your girl assistant, who stands facing the audience. You then take one end of the rope and another assistant, or, if you like, someone from the audience holds the other end.

When you give the word, both ends of the rope are pulled and the rope seems to cut right through the girl like wire cutting through a piece of cheese. But she doesn't fall apart, which is just as well.

How to do it

All you need for this illusion is a long piece of rope and a girl. You can do it with a boy if you like, but girls are nicer for the audience to look at.

The best kind of rope is white cotton clothes line and you want a piece about six yards long.

Begin by showing the rope and coiling it up, then throw it out to someone in the audience and ask him to pull on it to make sure it is strong. 'It has to be strong,' you explain, 'because I'm going to tie this young lady up with it and I don't want her to escape.'

Now take the rope by the centre part in both hands. Stand behind the girl and hold the rope in front of her by putting

your hands with the rope over her head. As you do this she puts her hands behind her back, which is quite a natural thing to do. And she holds one finger up straight behind her back at waist level.

Now bring the rope round her waist and apparently cross it behind her. What you really do is loop the right hand part of the rope over her finger then loop the left hand part over her finger and bring the ends of the rope round to the front. Have a look at Figure 1 and you'll see just what to do.

Now cross the rope in front of the girl's waist and give one end to your other assistant.

'I always use rope for this,' you say, 'because no girl likes to be had on a piece of string.'

You then go on to say, 'You've heard of a magician sawing through a woman. I have a much neater way of cutting girls up. I do it much the same way as the grocer cuts cheese, only I use a rope instead of wire.'

Then to your assistant holding the other end of the rope you say, 'When I say pull, you must pull hard on the rope. Make it a good strong pull because she's a pretty tough girl. Ready? Pull.'

The moment you say pull, the girl draws her finger out of the rope and the rope will appear to pull right through her. You must be careful not to have the rope held so tightly that she can't get her finger out. She may find it helpful to hold up both her first fingers and have the rope put round both of them. She can then hold the fingers slightly apart to take the pull of the rope and will then find it easy to release them.

As the rope pulls clear of the girl you say to her 'Shake yourself.' She does so and you remark, 'If the girl falls apart the trick is a failure.'

Making a Puffin

THE MORE PUFFIN' THE BETTER THE PUFFIN

You show a sheet of paper about eighteen inches by twelve and a number of smaller pieces of paper of different colours. 'With these pieces of paper,' you say, 'I am going to make a Puffin.'

You lay the big piece of paper on your table and put the small pieces on top. Then you fold the big piece of paper into a small packet with the coloured pieces inside.

'All you need to make a Puffin is some paper and some magic,' you say. 'The paper is easy, you just find it. The magic isn't so easy but I'll show you how it works.'

You hold up the folded packet. 'The magic consists of blowing on the paper.' You blow on it. Then you say, 'Would somebody else like a blow?' You hold it out for several people to blow on it. 'Puff away,' you say, 'the more puffin' the better the Puffin.'

You then open the paper and the audience see that the pieces of coloured paper have stuck themselves to the big sheet to make a picture of a Puffin.

18

How to do it

You take two of the big pieces of paper and you stick them together by a dab of paste on the centre. Now on one piece make a picture of a Puffin by cutting pieces of coloured paper and sticking them down. You'll find it easier if you draw the outline of your Puffin in pencil first. You can copy this from the Puffin on the cover of this book. Don't worry

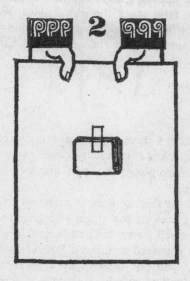

if your Puffin looks a bit wobbly. You can always say that some of the people puffed a bit crooked.

Now fold the sheet of paper with the Puffin on it into a small packet. Press the folds down well so that the packet will stay folded. If it doesn't want to stay put, stick a small piece of sticky tape over the edge to hold it.

You now have a large sheet of paper with the Puffin paper packet stuck to the back. Figure 2.

To perform the trick, hold up the paper, taking care not to expose the packet on the back. Lay it on your table and put the pieces of coloured paper on top. Fold the large sheet round the pieces, making a packet the same size as the hidden one. Stick a piece of sticky tape on this to hold it if that's what you did with the hidden one. You can now hold the two packets as one. When you blow on it you turn it over so that the Puffin picture comes on top. When you open the top one at the end of the trick you will discover the Puffin picture and the plain sheet with the pieces will be concealed. If you have stuck the packet with tape you just snip the tape with scissors, snipping of course the Puffin picture side, not the plain sheet by mistake, otherwise oo-er and things.

ANYONE CAN DO IT IF THEY HAVE THE MONEY

Change please

This is an entirely different trick from the Puffin trick but strangely enough it is done in exactly the same way. But that's magic.

You have a piece of paper, not a big piece this time, but a reasonably skinny little piece about three or four inches square. Ordinary writing paper will do. You borrow a ten penny piece from some horribly wealthy person in the audience, or from some very trusting person, and wrap it in the paper.

'I learnt this trick from the shops,' you explain. 'You know when you buy something in a shop and you don't happen to have the positively exactly right money, they very kindly give you change. It's not a bit clever of them really. Anyone can do it if they have the money. You just say "Change Please" and the job's done.'

You unwrap the ten penny piece and the audience see that it has changed to two five penny pieces.

'I hope you don't mind having your money changed,' you say to the person who lent you the ten penny piece, as you hand over the coins. 'But you get it all back, I don't charge for the magic.'

How to do it

You have a second piece of paper just like the first and they are stuck together by the centres, just as the big pieces were in the Puffin trick. Fold up the two five penny pieces in one piece and fix the packet with sticky tape.

Now you just wrap the ten penny piece in the paper, stick the packet with tape and secretly turn the two packets over while you are talking about the shop. When you open the packet you open the one with the change in it and there you are. But don't keep the prepared paper in your hand when you give the coins to the person who lent you the money. If you do somebody may say, 'Let's have a look at the paper.'

As you take out the two five penny pieces, carelessly screw up the paper and toss it into a box on your table. But don't forget there's a ten penny piece in it, will you? As if you would.

It would be quite a crafty idea to have a duplicate piece of paper in your box, folded like the piece you have used for the trick, only of course a single piece, and then unfolded again. Put some sticky tape on it so that it looks just like the piece you have been using.

After you have returned the coins, you go to the box to get something for the next trick, and you toss out this piece of paper, letting it fall on the floor near the audience. Someone will be sure to pick it up and look at it in the hope of finding out how you did the coin trick. But of course they won't discover. Clever you!

Visiting day

For this you want four saucers, three plain ones and one with a pattern, and four small pieces of tissue paper, all the same colour.

You crumple the pieces of tissue paper into four little balls and put one under each saucer. 'I want you to imagine,' you say, 'that the paper ball living in Rose Cottage * has invited the other balls of paper to tea.' You lift the first plain saucer and take out the ball of paper. 'Here is Mrs Ball of No. 1 The Avenue. She went off on her bicycle.' You make the ball of paper disappear, lift the patterned saucer and show there are now two paper balls there. 'Here she is at Rose Cottage.'

'Then Tessie Tissue of The White House trotted round on her feet.' You make the ball of paper from the second saucer vanish and that too appears under the patterned saucer. 'That leaves only Madam Paper from the end house.

* Call this saucer by whatever name suits the pattern on it. I have assumed it has roses, but if it is a Willow Pattern saucer you call it Willow Cottage, or The Flowers if it has a mixed flower pattern, and so on.

23

She was a bit of a witch so she just flew over on her jet propelled broomstick.' You lift the third plain saucer and show there is no ball under it and then show that all four paper balls are under the patterned saucer.

How to do it

You begin by putting a ball of paper under the first plain saucer and a second ball under the second saucer. But when you come to the third saucer you don't really put the ball of paper under it at all. This is managed by what conjurers would call sleight of hand, but don't let that scare you – it's a very easy piece of sleight of hand.

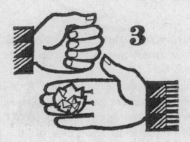

You pick up the paper ball with your right hand and hold it near the tips of the second and third fingers. In doing this you nip a bit of the paper between those two fingers. Now you appear to take the paper ball in your left hand. What you really do is to close your hand round the right hand fingers and at the same time turn your right hand with the back of it to the audience. Figure 3. Now move the closed left hand away, watching it as if it contained the ball, and nobody will know the ball isn't there, especially as they have no reason to expect anything unusual.

Now, keeping the paper ball concealed in your right hand, pick up the saucer with that hand, and pretend to put the ball under it with your left hand.

Now pick up the patterned saucer with your left hand and put it upside down in your right hand, holding the concealed paper ball against the inside of the saucer. Figure 4. Put the patterned saucer over the visible ball and leave the hidden one there with it.

You now have two paper balls under the patterned saucer but the audience think there is only one.

So far the audience think the trick hasn't begun, and you have just been arranging the articles for it. Now you explain how Mrs Ball from saucer number one set off. You lift the

4

saucer, take out the paper ball and apparently put it in your left hand. This is exactly the same piece of so-called sleight of hand I have already explained. But this time you make a throwing movement with your left hand towards the patterned saucer and show the hand empty. Lift the patterned saucer with your left hand and while everyone is looking at the two paper balls under it, put the patterned saucer upside down in your right hand, and over the concealed ball. Put the patterned saucer down over the two paper balls and add the third one, just as you did before.

That disposes of Mrs Ball. Tessie Tissue from saucer number two is vanished in exactly the same way, the patterned saucer is lifted to show three balls and the hidden one is again introduced under it. It is the same simple move over again.

As far as you are concerned, the trick is now over. All you have to do to make the last ball vanish is to make a pass over the third saucer and lift it to show there is no ball there. Remember, you didn't really put one there, so making a ball vanish that wasn't there to start with won't give you any trouble.

Finally you lift the patterned saucer, show the four balls of paper there, count them on to the saucer, stack the four saucers and put them aside.

A royal holiday

You take from a pack of cards the two red kings and the two red queens. 'These two royal couples', you say, 'were sharing the same palace so as to economize. They'd just had to give half of their kingdoms to chaps who'd slain dragons for them.'

You put the cards into a hat, or into a small box, to represent the palace.

'Of course the first thing the two queens decided to do was spring clean the palace, so the two kings reckoned it was time to go for a holiday. So off they went.' You take the two kings out of the box and put them back on top of the pack.

'But the queens weren't going to stay behind and do the spring cleaning. Not likely. They still had plenty of servants to do that. So they went off for a holiday too.' You turn the box or hat over and show that it is empty. The two queens have vanished. You then casually show the backs of the two red kings, in case anybody has awkward ideas about specially prepared cards.

How to do it

Anybody who has ideas about specially prepared cards will be quite right, but they won't know it because of the way you do the trick.

Take the king of diamonds and lay him on his face on the table. Now take a king and queen of diamonds and a queen of hearts from another pack of the same kind. Cut these three cards and stick them to the back of the king of diamonds as shown in Figure 5. Take a plain king of

hearts. If you now hold the two kings together with the faked side of the king of diamonds showing, they will look like four cards, the two red kings and two red queens. You hold them of course with the faked card behind the plain king of hearts.

Put them into the hat or box, being careful not to expose the back of the faked card.

When you take out the two kings, you show them with their ordinary faces to the front, holding the plain king of hearts behind the faked card. Put them back on the pack. But you secretly turn the pack over while you are taking the cards from the hat, so that the cards really go face down on the bottom of the pack.

Tell your story about the royal holiday and as you show the hat empty, secretly turn the pack over again. You have previously put a duplicate king of hearts and king of diamonds on top of the pack so you can now take these ordinary cards off and casually show them on both sides, leaving the audience with no clue to the mystery.

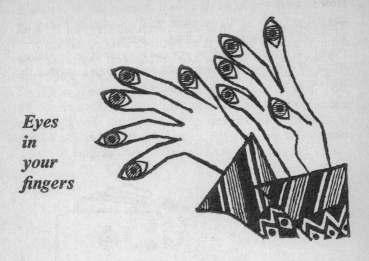

*Eyes
in
your
fingers*

This is a very easy trick with cards, but done well it produces a most uncanny effect on an audience.

You give the pack to four or five people and ask each one to take out a card and look at it but not to let you see what it is. You then collect these cards and shuffle them into the pack. After that you drop the pack into a hat, or a box, cover it with a handkerchief and shake the cards up. You can, if you like, get someone in the audience to shake the cards up, saying something like, 'Would someone else like to have a bit of a shake? It's rather like stirring the Christmas pudding, only quite different.'

Now you ask the first person who chose a card to name it. You show your hands empty, take a card out of the box and sure enough it is the one named. You do this with all the cards that were chosen, picking each one out of the covered box as it is named. Then you tip the rest of the cards out and the trick is over.

How to do it

This appears to be an absolute impossibility, yet it is all done with, what do you think? A little wire paper clip.

When you have had the four or five cards chosen, put the pack on your table and secretly pick up the wire paper clip. Now collect the chosen cards, with the faces down, of course, so that you can't see what they are. Then as you go to your table for the rest of the pack, you slide the paper clip on. Do this with the long end of the paper clip underneath, that is, next to the faces of the cards, Figure 6.

You can now shuffle the little packet of cards into the pack and have the cards shaken up in the box as much as you like. The chosen cards will remain clipped in a packet.

Now to find the chosen cards. When you collected the cards, you began with the first one chosen, then took the second one and put it on top of the first and so on. So you know that the first person's card will be at the bottom of the packet. And you also know that the bottom of the packet is where the long arm of the paper clip is. You can feel this quite easily.

Say to the first person, 'Will you tell me what card you

chose? The king of clubs?' (or whatever it happens to be).
'A very nice card, here it is.' You draw off the bottom card
of the packet, show it and drop it on the table. Now you ask
for the name of the second card. 'Three of diamonds? That's
very easy to find, the diamonds are so spiky.' You produce
the next card and so on for all four or five cards. Finally
tip out the cards, keeping the paper clip in your hand and
disposing of it behind the things on your table when you put
the box down.

Find the card

This effective trick consists of making a member of the audience pick out of the pack, which you have put in his pocket, a card chosen by a member of the audience. It is a good trick to follow the one called, 'Eyes in your finger tips,' because it is a similar effect, done in quite a different way, and done by a member of the audience, apparently.

How to do it

Take a pack of cards to someone in the audience and ask him to choose one, look at it and be sure to remember what card it is. He will probably take elaborate precautions to prevent your catching sight of it. Let him enjoy himself, because you don't need to know what the card is.

Now lift off about half the cards with your right hand and hold out the lower half, asking him to put his card on it. You then apparently put the other half on top and shuffle the card into the pack. Actually you do nothing of the kind. What you do is to bring your hand down and tap the lower half of the pack with the top half, then shuffle all the top cards off under the bottom half. Figure 7 will explain how to do this. Now you give the cards another shuffle. To

do this you take about half the cards off the top again. But you press lightly on the top card, which is of course the chosen one, and so cause this card to stay on the lower

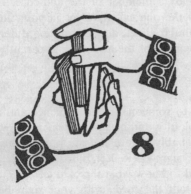

half of the pack as you draw the top half off. Figure 8. Conjurers call this slipping a card. It's as easy as shuffling a pack of cards, and if you can't shuffle a pack of cards you can't very well expect to do card tricks.

You have now apparently shuffled the pack well but, un-known to the audience, the chosen card is on the top. You now ask someone in the audience to help you. But whatever you do, don't say, 'Now I want someone in the audience to help me with this piece of magic.' If you say that you'll have the entire audience on the stage. That is if your audience consists of children. What you must do is pick out a boy who is wearing a jacket. That is essential to the trick. And try to pick a boy who looks friendly and not the kind who might try to be smart and spoil the show. It makes things easier for you and more enjoyable for the audience if you can pick the right kind of boy. But it isn't likely to affect the trick because he can't spoil the effect even if he tries. All he will be able to do is make himself look rather silly if he tries to be smart.

Having got your helper on to the stage you say 'Have you got an inside pocket in your jacket? I should like to borrow it if I may. Don't tear it out, I'll use the pocket just where it is, but I'd like you to take out anything that is in the pocket.'

This will probably result in the boy taking out of his pocket several yards of string, a half eaten packet of choco-late, three white mice, seven assorted marbles, the bits of a model aeroplane, one or two comics and a handful of chalks. In any case you can say, 'It's surprising what people carry in their pockets nowadays,' and make some remark on whatever he does take out.

You then put the pack of cards into his pocket. Take care that the backs of the cards face the front of his jacket. 'I'm going to ask this gentleman,' you say to the audience, 'to discover and take out of the pack the very card this other gentleman chose,' (or lady, if a girl chose the card). Then ask the boy with the pack in his pocket to touch the chooser of the card lightly on the head with his right hand, 'To absorb knowledge of the card', as you put it. 'Just a gentle touch,' you explain, 'no clouting, we don't want to start a war.'

You then go on talking to the boy with the pack in his pocket. 'I want you to touch this gentleman's forehead, then quickly put your hand in your pocket and take out his card. But remember you must be quick. Touch his forehead, then quick, into your pocket and take out the card.'

What will happen is that the boy will pull out of his pocket the first card that comes to hand. This will naturally be the one on the top of the pack because that is the easiest one to take out. That is why you make him do it quickly. You give him no time to get hold of a card out of the middle of the pack.

So, he puts his hand into his pocket, brings out a card, and wowsie! or other magical remarks, it jolly well is the chosen card.

Of course there is just a chance that he may not bring out the right card. He may for some reason take out some other card, or he may deliberately take a card out of the middle of the pack to try to spoil the trick. If he does, it doesn't matter. You just say 'Ah, I told you that you had to be quick. You let the influence of this gentleman's thoughts evaporate. Let me show you.' Saying this you lightly touch the card-chooser's forehead, plunge your hand into the boy's pocket and of course bring out the top card of the pack, which is the chosen one.

THY SLIGHTEST WISH OH MASTER IS TO ME AS THE STERNEST COMMAND

The obedient card

Here is a card trick with an unusual effect. You have a card chosen and shuffle it into the pack, then you make it appear at any position in the pack chosen by the person who took the card.

How to do it

Have a card chosen and put back in the same way as that described for 'Find the Card'. Shuffle the pack, pressing on the top card, which is of course the chosen one, just as you did in 'Find the Card'.

You now have the pack with the chosen card on top although of course nobody but you knows it is there.

Now, speaking to the person who chose the card, you say, 'The card you chose now regards you as its master and will do what you tell it. Of course you musn't tell it to do anything too difficult, like making a rice pudding or cycling up the curtains. I suggest you tell it to move itself to whatever position in the pack you would like it to be. Say tenth from the top, or eighth from the top. Would you like to suggest how many your card should be from the top? Don't make it more than fifty-two, will you?'

Suppose the chooser of the card says he wants it seventh from the top. You go on 'Seventh from the top? That's fine, but first of all we'd better make sure it isn't already seventh from the top, as it might be by some coincidence, because in that case there would be no magic.' You deal the cards on to the table from the top of the pack, laying them down with the backs up, count up to seven and show the seventh card, which will not of course be the chosen one. 'Right,' you say, 'we can now get your servant to perform.' You pick up the cards and put them back on top of the pack.

Now, in counting them you put the top card, which is the chosen one, down first and counted the others on top. It is the natural way to count them. But this means that if you count off seven cards, what was the top one is now seventh. You put this little packet back on the pack and so bring the chosen card to seventh. Of course it works just as well whatever number is chosen.

Now all you have to do is to ask the chooser of the card to tell it to pass to seventh from the top. Count them off, then when you come to the seventh, ask him to name his card, and turn it up. Of course, it is the card he chose.

Radio post

This is quite a showy card trick and very mysterious. You begin by asking someone to come up and help you. You seat him on a chair to your left and run through a pack of cards so that he can see it is an ordinary pack, 'They aren't made up of pictures of sweet little doggies, you will notice,' you say, 'and most of them are quite clean.'

You then count off half the cards on to his hand, ask him to turn them face to face and tie round them a piece of ribbon, which you give him.

You then go to two other persons in the audience, spread the other half of the pack in front of them in turn and ask them to think of a card each. 'Don't tell me which one you're thinking of,' you say, 'but just think of one of the cards you can see, and remember it.

'I am now going to send these cards by radio post to the other half of the pack which this gentleman is holding so securely,' you announce. 'For this I need my Radio Post Transmitter.' You pick up a little black box with some wire attached. 'I shall just aim the Radio Post Transmitter at each of the persons who thought of a card,' you say, 'but don't be alarmed, it doesn't hurt as much as ordinary radio, in fact you won't feel a thing.' You point the box at the two people concerned and if you can arrange to have a little buzzer in the box, you can buzz it for effect.

'I now turn the Radio Post Transmitter on to the half of the pack this gentleman is holding,' you say. You buzz the box at him.

You then ask the two people who thought of the cards to say what they were, and you show that these cards have vanished. Tell the gentleman holding the other part of the pack to untie the ribbon and see if the thought-of cards have arrived, and to take them out and hold them up.

Sure enough he finds the cards and holds them up.

How to do it

Although this seems such a miracle there is not actually a single difficult thing to do. And no special cards are used. But you will need two packs alike. You also want a short piece of ribbon and a little black box with a bit of wire on it, got up to look like some sort of radio thing. Or you can simply use an electric torch.

To prepare for the trick, count off half the cards from one pack and lay the other twenty-six aside. I'll tell you what to do with them presently.

From the other pack, take out the twenty-six cards that are the same as the twenty-six you have counted from the other pack. You now have a pack of fifty-two cards which is really two half packs the same.

This is the pack you show to the person who comes to help. Run through the cards to let him see that they are apparently all different. Don't say a word about no cards being repeated because if you do he'll look to see if any are repeated and you'll give the trick away. Just make some remark about the cards being clean or very spotty. He will not be able to notice that the pack is made up of two halves alike, and the audience will of course assume that the pack is ordinary because they will think the chap helping you would notice anything special about it.

Now count the top twenty-six cards on to his hand, ask him to put them face to face and tie them with the ribbon you give him.

Take the other half of the pack in turn to two people in the audience and ask them each to think of one of the cards. Of course it doesn't matter what cards they think of because the duplicates of all the cards they can see are already in the other half of the pack. But of course you must be sure they think of one of the cards they can see. You can be certain of this by saying, 'I want you to think of one of these cards as I run through them. Just think of a card, don't tell which card you think of.'

Having done that, you must now secretly change this half pack for a half pack consisting of the twenty-six cards you haven't used so far. When you run through these, the two cards thought of will of course be missing.

This is how we make the exchange. It is really the reason why you use what you call your Radio Post Transmitter. You have this thing, or an ordinary pocket torch, if that is what you are going to use, in a shoe box on your table. And in the box, against the torch, is the other half of the pack of cards. That is to say the half of the pack containing the twenty-six cards you haven't used yet.

You say, 'I will now show you my Radio Post Transmitter. It's a queer kind of radio thing and it transmits actual objects instead of just sounds.' So saying, you put your right hand, in which you are holding the half pack of cards, into the box. You leave that half pack in the box and pick up the torch and the other half pack together and bring them out. To make it look natural for you to take the torch out of the box with the hand that holds the cards, instead of using your other hand, you can take your handkerchief out of your pocket with your left hand, and rub your nose with it.

The trick is now done as far as you are concerned, but to the audience it has only just started.

You announce that you are going to use your Radio Post Transmitter to transmit the cards the two people thought of to the other half of the pack the gentleman is holding. Shine the torch, or aim the box thing, first at one of the people who thought of a card, then at the person holding the half pack. Then aim it at the other card-thinker-of and again at the person holding the pack. Do this as if you really thought it was making the cards travel to the other half of the pack. In fact you should say to yourself, 'There goes one card,' and then, 'there goes the other card.' It makes a trick much more convincing if the conjurer looks as if he believes in it himself.

Now to show that the thought-of cards have gone. You say, 'We'll get an independent witness to see that the cards have really gone,' and you go to someone sitting some little distance from the two people who thought of the cards. This appears to make the trick if anything more difficult because it rules out any idea the audience might have that you had arranged beforehand with the people who thought of the cards, what cards to say they'd thought of. But really you go to another person some distance away so that the people who thought of the cards will not notice that all the cards you now show are different from those they saw before. This is a necessary precaution, because in looking at the cards in the first place, to think of one, these people are sure to notice one or two other cards.

'Nobody knows as yet what cards these two people thought of,' you say, 'except the people concerned. Will you please say what card you thought of?' Suppose it was the ace of hearts. Then to the other person, 'And your card? The king of spades.' Of course it may be any two cards, I just name these to make my description clear.

To the person you have referred to as an independent witness you now show the cards. In fact you can put the half pack into his hands. 'Will you go through these cards and make sure that the ace of hearts and king of spades' (or whichever two cards they were) 'have left this half of the pack.'

Of course the cards will be missing. You then ask the gentleman holding the half pack tied with ribbon to undo the ribbon, find the two cards and hold them up for the audience to see.

This remarkable trick was originally invented and performed by David Devant, the greatest magician who ever lived. He was one of the partners in the famous firm of Maskelyne and Devant, of whom you may not have heard, but your parents will almost certainly know the names and may even have seen David Devant perform. The version of the trick I have described is simplified to make it convenient for you to do. I hope you will take care to learn to do it well. It is a great piece of magic and should bring you lots of applause.

Silk from nowhere

When you are going to use a silk handkerchief in a trick, it's much more magical to produce it from nowhere, rather than just pick it up off your table. There are several ways of doing this.

Number One Way. Roll up the handkerchief and tuck in the end to make a neat little parcel. Put this little parcel under your left arm. You will find you can hold it there quite comfortably. No need to strain yourself and look as if your elbow is chained to your body.

You face the audience and say, 'For my first item I use nothing at all.'* Extend your right hand and with the left hand draw up your sleeve. You do this by putting your left hand under the upper part of your right arm, thumb on

---

* This is best done as your first trick as you can't go about for long with the handkerchief under your arm.

top and finger underneath. You say, 'Nothing in my right hand.' Now show the left hand empty and draw up the left sleeve with the right hand in the same way. This brings the hidden balled-up handkerchief very naturally into your right hand, where you keep it concealed.

'And nothing in my left hand. I just put those two nothings together and get one something.' As you say this you put your hands together and shake out the handkerchief.

Number Two Way. Twist the handkerchief ropewise, wind it round your right thumb and tuck in the end. You can now show your hands empty by spreading out the fingers, flat on

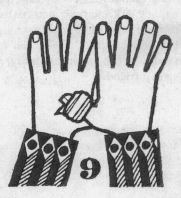

to the audience, and keeping the right thumb, with the handkerchief on it, behind the left hand. Figure 9. Now turn your hands over, sliding your right thumb down behind the fingers, then unroll the handkerchief.

'For this piece of magic I use two hands. It's easier with three hands but they only gave me two. I put the two hands together and get one handkerchief.'

Number Three Way. This is very sensational. The handkerchief seems to appear suddenly in mid air and float into your hands. It isn't difficult to do but you'll find you need a little practice to get it just right.

The handkerchief is crumpled up into a small ball but no ends are tucked in, it is just left loose. The crumpled ball is then placed in the bend of your left elbow and you draw a fold of your sleeve over it to cover it. Come forward with your hands clasped in front of you. This gives you an excuse to keep your arms bent. Say, 'I don't know whether you've noticed, but the air in this room is full of things floating about. You probably can't see them, but to a magician they're very noticeable. I'll see if I can make one of them visible.'

As you say this you clap your hands and suddenly straighten both arms directly towards the audience. Do this with a quick jerk and the concealed handkerchief will be shot out from the bend of your elbow so quickly nobody will see where it comes from. It will open out in the air and float down and you can catch it daintily, rather like a cart horse waving to a friend.

**SO SMOOTH!
SO UNSPILL-
ABLE!**

Silk soup

Now that you've produced a silk handkerchief from nowhere, you should do some magic with it. So you show a soup plate and lay it upside down on a sheet of newspaper.

'I'm going to turn this silk handkerchief into a sort of silk soup,' you say. 'Just watch the handkerchief and you'll see it turn into soup.' You throw the handkerchief into the air and it vanishes. And when you lift the soup plate there it is.

'One advantage of that kind of soup,' you remark, 'is that it doesn't spill on your waistcoat.'

How to do it

First, how to produce the silk handkerchief, really another one that looks the same, of course, from under the soup plate.

On the table to your right is a sheet of newspaper. Under the back edge of the newspaper is the silk handkerchief you are going to make appear under the soup plate. It should be folded corners into the middle several times to make a small bundle. The bundle is not fixed in any way, but just placed under the back edge of the newspaper. On top of the newspaper put an ordinary soup plate. The weight of the plate will stop the silk from unrolling.

Having produced your silk as I have already explained, lay it on another table. Now with your left hand slide the

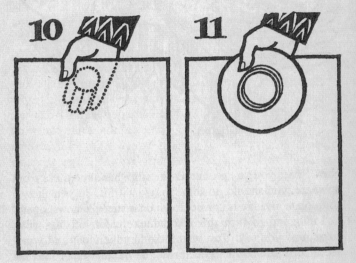

soup plate forward on the newspaper. At the same time pick up the newspaper with your right hand, holding it by the back edge. You will then be able to get hold of the folded silk and hold it concealed behind the paper. Figure 10. You now have the soup plate in your left hand and the newspaper in your right. Show both sides of the paper. Your hand will keep the silk concealed. Now show both sides of the soup plate. Place the plate upside down on top of the newspaper and grip it with your right hand. Figure 11. Now with your left hand draw the newspaper away, leaving the hidden silk now concealed under the plate.

Lay the newspaper on the table and put the soup plate, upside down, on top of it. You put the front edge of the plate down first, then let the back edge drop on to the paper. This leaves the silk under the plate.

But how do you make the other silk vanish in mid air? Trained canaries waiting to fly off with it? Yards of elastic to haul it up your sleeve? Nothing so difficult. Pick up the handkerchief by one corner with your right hand and hold it up for everyone to see. While attention is drawn to the silk, your left hand takes hold of the lapel of your jacket (you must wear a jacket for this effect) and opens it slightly. Now you make a throwing up and down movement with the silk, saying, 'Just watch the handkerchief and you'll see it turn into soup.' You then apparently throw the handkerchief into the air. To do this you bring your hand down and back, throw the silk under your coat and immediately bring your left arm in to your side to hold the silk. Continue the throwing movement and follow it with your eyes. To the audience the silk seems to vanish in mid air. Try this a few times in front of a mirror to get the timing right. It's quite easy but it needs a few practice tries.

All you now have to do is pick up the plate with your right hand and show the silk under it. Gather up plate, paper and silk and carry them behind your screen, or whatever you use for a behind-the-scenes, where you can get rid of the handkerchief under your coat.

HELP!
I'M
BEING
FRAMED

Wild animals

This is not a description of how to vanish a tiger or cause an elephant to float up to the ceiling. I hope you aren't disappointed. You'll see presently why I call it by this name.

You begin by showing a photo frame. It is one of those frames made from cardboard, covered with leather paper. The cardboard is double and the photo together with a piece of transparent sort of stuff is slid in between the thicknesses of cardboard. Frames like this are quite cheap, or you could even make one. Have a photo of yourself in the frame.

'This photograph frame has one peculiarity,' you say, 'I expect you can see what that peculiarity is, a photo of me.' You now ask someone in the audience to come forward and take the frame. 'Will you take out the awful picture, and the transparent material and make sure that there are no other horrid things concealed in it.' You then take back the empty frame, slide the transparent material back and wrap the frame in a sheet of newspaper.

'I'd like you to hold this wrapped-up frame,' you say to your assistant. 'And don't let me touch it. If I should come near it before the end of the trick, please shout "Fire" or "Homework" or something equally alarming. Now I want someone to call out the name of a wild animal, any wild animal, come on shout. Lion did you say? All right, a lion it shall be.' To the person holding the frame, 'Will you take off the wrapping and see what has arrived in the frame.'

Your assistant unwraps the frame and there, filling it, is a picture of a lion. 'Don't be frightened, he won't bite.' You take the picture out of the frame, or let your assistant do it.

How to do it

You need two frames exactly alike. One of them, in which you have put a nice picture of a lion, is on your table, between the sheets of a folded piece of newspaper, the fold

being at the back. Under this paper are two or three other similar folded sheets of newspaper. If you look at the diagram, Figure 12, which shows a sort of edge-on view of the papers, you will see that the two halves of the top sheet and the top half of the second sheet are pulled out a little and turned up. This is so that you can pick up all three of these thicknesses of paper together.

When you have had the visible frame emptied and put together again, you go to your table to wrap the frame in paper. You do this by apparently lifting the top half of the

51

folded sheet, slipping the frame in and picking up frame and paper by the folded edge. What you really do is this. You pick up the two edges of the top folded piece and the top edge of the second piece, all together. You put the frame under them, so it goes into the folded piece of paper that is second from the top. Figure 13. You let the papers drop on top of the frame, then you pick up the top folded piece,

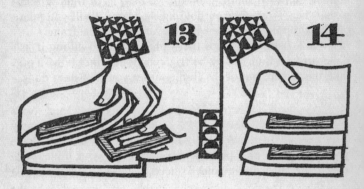

gripping the hidden frame through them, as in Figure 14, and hand the parcel to your assistant, folding the paper round the frame as you do so. This folding the paper round the frame is necessary because it prevents your assistant from looking at the frame before you are ready for him to do so. The extra sheets of newspaper on the table are there to disguise the fact that you have two sheets of paper. By having several sheets it just looks as if you had a few sheets of newspaper ready to wrap things in.

Now all you have to do is to ask for the name of a wild animal and so bring the trick to its conclusion.

'Stop!' I can hear you cry. 'Give us our tuppence back. That's no good. Suppose someone doesn't call out "Lion", suppose they say "Tiger" or "Elephant" or name some other animal?'

Well, I'll tell you in a minute what to do if that should

happen. But first let me tell you something else. If you ask an audience to name a wild animal, it's forty thousand Puffins to a second-hand acid drop that someone will call out 'lion'. It's the first wild animal anyone thinks of. That's why you use a photo of a lion. And if someone does call out 'lion' as they probably will do, that makes the trick look like a real piece of magic because the audience will wonder how you could possibly conjure a picture of an animal into the frame when you didn't know what animal anyone might call out.

But suppose nobody does call out 'lion' or suppose someone with a very loud shouting sort of voice insists on shouting the name of some other animal? What do you do? Have him thrown out? Pour a glass of water down his neck? Or just say, as if repeating what he said, 'This gentleman wants a lion.' As a matter of fact I've known conjurers get away with things as cheeky as that before now. But you don't have to worry. If somebody calls out the name of the wrong animal, you pick up a little scribbling pad and a pencil and you start writing down the names of the animals the audience calls out. Only you really write 'Lion' on every sheet. The audience don't know this of course, and now and again you should check your spelling by saying some-such things as, 'How many f's in elephant?' During this calling out someone is sure to call out 'lion' and even if they don't nobody will remember that nobody has.

When you have had six or seven names called out and written 'Lion' every time while pretending to write down the names called out, you actually do write down the last name that is called out. Suppose this is Kangaroo. Then you go to someone in the front row and say, 'I want to make sure you can read my writing. I can't read it myself, so I want to be sure someone can. Would you mind reading what I have written here.' The person addressed will naturally read out 'Kangaroo', which makes it look as if you had written down different names all the time.

Now take the sheets of paper and turn them over so that the writing is underneath, fold back the bottom paper and ask the person who read out 'Kangaroo' to take one. Of course he's bound to get one with 'Lion' written on it and you then proceed with the trick.

Making time fly

This is a trick with a borrowed watch, in which you can have a bit of fun with the person who trusts you with his watch.

Described very briefly, the trick goes like this. You borrow a gentleman's hat, show that it is empty and put it on a table. Then you borrow a watch, wrap it in tissue paper and put it into a glass. You then proceed to make first the watch, then the tissue paper and finally the glass disappear. After that you produce them one at a time from the hat.

How you do it

You probably know that when a magician makes something disappear and finds it somewhere else, he usually has two of those somethings, both alike. The one he produces from somewhere else is not the one that he made disappear. Well that is part of the secret of this piece of magic. But of course it can't explain the watch, can it? I mean you borrow a watch, you make it vanish and then you produce the same watch from the hat. You couldn't very well have lined up

55

behind the scenes exact duplicates of all the watches that might be offered to you for the trick.

But we're dashing ahead too quickly. Let's begin at the beginning, which is a very good starting place.

On your table is a large sheet of tissue paper loosely folded. On the edge of it lies a small tumbler, preferably one of those transparent plastic ones which won't get broken and so mess up the trick. In this tumbler is a square of tissue paper the same colour as the big sheet. This square of paper is twisted up to look as if it contained something, and tucked

loosely into the tumbler. The rest of the tissue paper is then folded forward and then back so that it hides the tumbler. The front edge of the big sheet of paper must be held down. A good way is to have the paper arranged to conceal the tumbler, on a tray, and tuck the front edge of the sheet of tissue paper under the tray. Figure 15. You'll see why this front edge has to be held, in a moment.

Also on the table is a duplicate of the small tumbler.

First you borrow a gentleman's hat. And it's just as well to have a suitable hat, a nice stiff one, given to someone in the audience before the show, with instructions to hand it up when you ask for a hat, if nobody else offers one. This is just a precaution in case nobody in the audience has a hat, which might happen in the summer.

You show the hat empty, then you hold it by the brim in your left hand and go to your table, which should be on your right. With your right hand you pick up the big sheet of tissue paper. In doing this you will find it quite easy to make the hidden tumbler roll into the hat. Figure 16. The held-down front edge of the paper helps here.

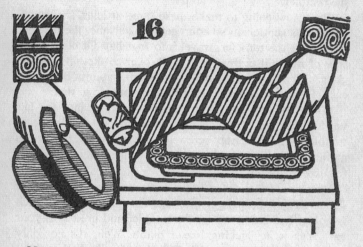

Now you walk over to another table and put the hat down. To the audience the hat is still empty.

Now, still holding the tissue paper, you ask someone to lend you a watch. 'I should like a nice expensive watch, please,' you say, 'the more expensive the watch the better the trick.' Somebody holds up a watch. You say rather quickly, 'Don't throw it, I'll come and get it.'

You go and get the watch and return to your stage, holding the watch up for all to see. You then tear a piece off the sheet of tissue paper. You have previously prepared the sheet by creasing it sharply so that you can easily tear off a piece the same size as the piece in the glass, which is now in the hat. You discard the rest of the paper and proceed, very openly, to wrap the borrowed watch in the small piece.

While you are doing this you say something like, 'I'm going to wrap the watch in tissue paper, then if anything awful happens to it, it won't be my fault.'

Take the wrapped watch, pick up the small tumbler, which you will remember is on the table from which you took the sheet of tissue paper. Put the wrapped watch into the tumbler.

'I am now going to make these three articles, the watch, which this gentleman so courageously lent me, the piece of paper and the tumbler, travel into that hat. Of course one way of doing it is this.' You walk over to the hat, put the glass in it and at once take it out again, saying, 'But that's easy. Even you could do it. There's no magic in that.'

When you put the glass, watch and paper into the hat you didn't take it out again. You took out the duplicate tumbler with the empty screwed up paper in it. But to the audience the trick hasn't started yet so they have no reason to suspect anything.

Now you go to your other table and put the tumbler down. Say to the person who lent the watch, 'Your watch is going, I hope?' Pick up the tumbler and hold it to your ear. 'Yes it is. Ticking like a bomb. Well, it's not only going, it'll soon be gone.' This by-play is to keep the audience thinking that the watch is still in the tumbler. You make a pass towards the hat, 'There goes your watch, sir.' You take out the paper, unwrap it and show that the watch has gone.

Now for the tumbler. To do this part of the trick you have the cloth on your table pinned up with safety pins at the back to form a sort of bag. You lay the tissue paper over the tumbler and press it round so that the paper takes the shape of the tumbler. Now draw the tumbler back and apparently pick it up. What you really do is to draw the tumbler off the back edge of the table and let it slip out into the concealed bag. But the tissue paper keeps the shape as if the tumbler were still under it. Figure 17.

At this point you can introduce a very effective piece of misdirection. You don't have to do it, but if you do, it will make the vanishing of the tumbler much more astonishing. On your table is a small plate or saucer and behind it is a

17

coin. You hold the tissue paper, apparently covering the tumbler, in your left hand. You pick up the plate with your right hand and get the coin on to your fingers at the same time. Now hold the plate flat, your fingers with the coin resting on them are just below the plate. Appear to put the tissue paper covered glass on the plate. As you do this, bring the coin up against the under side of the plate. The coin clinking against the plate sounds exactly as if the covered glass were being put on the plate. You then squash the tissue paper down on the plate and show that the tumbler has gone.

Finally you make the tissue paper disappear by rolling it into a ball and making use of the moves described for the item called 'Visiting Day'.

'Watch, paper and tumbler all gone,' you say. 'Now let's see if they've arrived in the hat.' You pick up the hat and in doing so get rid of the ball of tissue paper that is concealed in your hand. You can just drop this behind some article on your table. Reach into the hat, letting everyone see that your hand is empty, tip the tumbler over and shake the wrapped watch out into the hat, then produce the tumbler. 'Well the tumbler's arrived. I'm glad of that because that was mine.' Now take out the tissue paper, unwrapping it and leaving the watch in the hat. 'And here's the tissue paper. It's all screwed up so I'll unscrew it so that you can see it properly. Very unscrewpulous, but conjurers are unscrupulous people, as the gentleman who lent me the watch is beginning to find out.'

You then work up a bit of fun by ignoring the watch and saying, 'Now if someone will lend me a still more expensive watch I'll show you something even better.' Then pretending to hear a protest from the owner of the watch, 'Oh, you want your watch back first? I was afraid of that.' Then to the audience, 'Aren't people unreasonable? Fancy lending a watch to a conjurer and expecting to get it back.'

You pick up the hat, peep in and move the hat round and round as if it contained some liquid. 'In order to pass your watch into the hat I had to melt it down,' you say. Then you appear to be struck with a sudden idea. You pick up the tumbler and appear to be going to pour something into it from the hat. 'I'll tell you what I'll do. I'll pour the watch into this tumbler, then you can drink it and you'll always know what the time is.'

This will get a laugh, and after the laughter has died down, which won't take more than an hour or so, you say, 'Well never mind, sir, I'll just cool your watch down.' You either blow into the hat, or fan it with a little fan. Then you lift the watch from the hat, letting everyone see that it is the same watch. 'There you are, sir, I return your watch with many thanks, and hearty congratulations on getting it back.'

Broken biscuits

Here is a trick that is quite simple to do, and if well done looks almost like a miracle.

You begin by offering a tin of biscuits to someone in the front row of the audience. You ask him to take one. 'Don't eat it,' you say. 'Sorry to disappoint you but I want you to break the biscuit into bits.' This your helper does and you collect the bits on a plate, saying, 'I'd like you to keep back one of the bits, and please keep it safely.'

You then smash up the rest of the biscuit into crumbs, and put them into an envelope which you ask another member of the audience to seal. 'I'll put the envelope full of biscuit crumbs into this glass dish,' you say. You do so and put the dish on a tray on your table.

'Of course anyone can smash up a biscuit,' you say. 'But only a magician would want to do such a ridiculous thing as make a smashed up biscuit whole again. So that's what I'm going to do.'

You make a pass over the envelope and hand it to someone in the audience to open. He finds in it the biscuit completely restored except for one piece. And the piece retained by the person who broke the biscuit fits the gap exactly. Which is quite impossible. Aren't you clever?

How to do it

For this trick you will need a small round tin with a loose lid. The tin contains a few biscuits, plain round ones, not too fragile. Marie biscuits are very suitable. Before the performance you take one biscuit and carefully break a small piece out. Put this piece on top of the tin of biscuits and leave the tin behind your screen.

Now put the biscuit with the piece broken out, into an envelope, seal it and lay it on your table just under the back edge of a small tray. Beside the tray have a glass bowl just big enough to take the envelope. You also want a packet of envelopes the same as the one under the tray, a small plate and something to crush the biscuit into crumbs. A dessert spoon will do.

You go behind your screen and bring on the tin of biscuits, holding it by the top with your right hand, which covers the little bit of biscuit on the lid. Take the tin in your left hand and remove the lid with your right. Offer the tin to someone in the front row and ask him, or her, of course, to take a biscuit and break it up. While this is being done put the tin and lid on your table, keeping the little bit of biscuit concealed in your right hand, and bring the plate forward to receive the pieces.

Now comes a very crafty piece of what conjurers call misdirection. When you say to the biscuit breaker, 'I want you to keep back one of the pieces,' you apparently pick up a piece of biscuit from the plate and give it to him. What you really do is pretend to pick up a piece and give him the piece in your hand. The audience, except those sitting each side of the one who takes the biscuit, will think that he kept hold of a piece of the biscuit and that you never touched it.

This will make the climax of the trick a great deal more astonishing.

Now take the plate of pieces, crush them up with the back of the spoon and pour the crumbs into one of the envelopes. Give this to someone in the audience to seal. You can be sure he'll have a good look at the envelope while doing this, so everyone will be quite satisfied that it is an ordinary envelope.

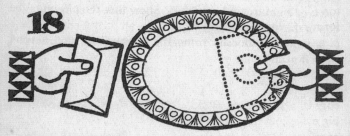

Take the envelope of crumbs with your left hand. Pick up the tray with the concealed envelope under it with your right hand. Figure 18. You now appear to put the tray into your left hand and transfer the envelope of crumbs to your right hand. If you try this with the articles in your hands

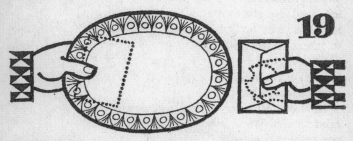

you'll find it quite difficult to do, but of course you don't really do that. What you do is this. You place the tray into your left hand, on top of the envelope of crumbs. Then you move your right hand away holding the envelope containing the biscuit. Figure 19. It looks so natural nobody will suspect that the envelope has been changed. Put the envelope into the glass bowl. Lay the tray on the table, where it hides the envelope of crumbs, and put the bowl on top.

All you now have to do is make mysterious passes over the envelope, and get someone to open it and find the restored biscuit. Take the biscuit from them and hold it up so that everyone can see there is a piece missing. Ask the chooser of the biscuit to give you what you refer to as, 'the piece of biscuit you kept back.' Show that the piece fits the gap in the biscuit.

If that trick doesn't bring the house down you haven't done it neatly.

TRICKS WITH SPECIAL THINGS
and how to make the things

Conjurer's handy box

Now we can go on to some rather more showy tricks in which special apparatus is used. All the special things you will need for these tricks you can make quite easily if you follow the directions. But do take care to make them neatly, and make them strong. And decorate them with paint or fancy paper so that they'll look attractive.

The first thing I want you to make is not actually used for a particular trick. But it is mighty useful helping you to do several tricks.

It is simply a box without a lid. It can be made of stout cardboard or wood. It should be about fifteen inches long, ten inches wide and eight inches deep. If you can find a nice clean box somewhere about this size, you won't have to make one. Figure 20.

Inside the box you fit a vertical partition about six inches from the front. This partition runs from end to end of the box and is about three inches high. In front of this partition place a soft folded cloth. This is for secretly dropping things

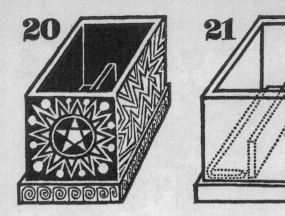

on when you want to get rid of them, and the folded cloth stops them from making a bump when you drop them. The space behind the partition is for things you want to take out during the show. Paint the box black inside. Figure 21.

If you are going to make the box, make it with the bottom about an inch and a half higher than the bottom would be in an ordinary box, so that you have a secret space under the box. If you are using an ordinary box you arrange this secret space by fastening strips of wood or card round the bottom of the box as shown in Figure 21.

Aunt Jane's knitting bag

'Of course everybody has an Aunt Jane,' you say, 'but my Aunt Jane was a special kind of aunt; special in two ways. She couldn't knit for nuts and she couldn't remember anything.'

'This is Aunt Jane's knitting bag,' you hold up a small red bag, 'in which she used to keep the knitting she couldn't do.' You take out some very scraggy looking knitting. 'And the stitches she used to drop.' You tip up the bag and a lot of white beads or beans fall out.

'One day Aunt Jane left her knitting bag on a bus, or in a train or on a park seat, or somewhere. She couldn't remember where. So she went to the Lost Property Office to see if they had it.

' "What colour bag is it?" asked the Lost Property Man.

' "A red one," said Aunt Jane, "with a black lining." ' You show the red bag and turn it inside out to show the black lining. Leave it like that and go on:

'The Lost Property Man looked everywhere but couldn't find a red bag anywhere. "Oh," said Aunt Jane, "perhaps it wasn't red, it might have been blue." ' You turn the bag right

69

side out and the audience see that it isn't red but blue. ' "But I know it had a black lining," said Aunt Jane.' You turn the bag inside out again and the lining is still black.

You then go on telling the story of Aunt Jane and the bag changes colour every time you turn it, but the lining stays black.

'The Lost Property Man had another look but couldn't find a blue bag either. "We.e.e.ell," murmured Aunt Jane, "it could just possibly be gold. But the lining is definitely black."'

'However there was no gold bag in the Lost Property Office, so Aunt Jane admitted it might have been green, but she insisted that it had a black lining.'

'But there was no green bag. Aunt Jane then thought it might have been purple with a black lining.'

'And when eventually Aunt Jane's knitting bag was found, it turned out to be a striped one, and the lining was white.' You turn the bag for the last time, it becomes striped and when turned inside out it has a white lining.

How to do it

The whole trick of course depends on a specially made bag, so I'll show you how to make the bag.

First you persuade Mum to let you have a go at the bag or box in which she keeps forty thousand pieces of all kinds of stuff in case it should come in useful one of these days. You just explain that this is one of those days and away you go. If Mum doesn't have any pieces, which will be so unlikely as to be almost impossible, you'll have to save up the old pocket money and buy some. A cheap satin is best. You'll want several colours, also a piece of striped material of some kind.

Cut each piece of material to about eighteen inches by seven inches. The exact size is not important but they must all be the same size.

70

Now you want some pieces of black ribbon or tape about an inch wide and seven inches long.

Lay one end of the red piece of material against one end of the striped piece and bind them together with one of the pieces of tape, sewing them neatly. Now lay the unbound end of the striped piece against one end of the green piece and bind them together with tape. Bind the unbound end of the green piece to one end of the yellow piece. Continue binding the ends of the pieces together like this, using the black piece next, then the blue piece and finally the white piece. Figure 22 shows how the pieces should look from an end-on view.

Now bring the unbound end of the red piece right round all the pieces and bind it to the unbound end of the white piece. The affair should now look like Figure 23.

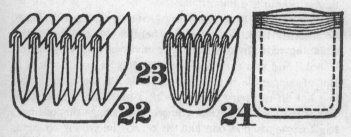

What you now have is a series of differently coloured bags sewn together at the top but with the sides open. The next thing to do is to sew right through all the thicknesses, down one side, across the bottom and up the other side, as shown in Figure 24. Make sure you sew all the thicknesses together all the way round, especially at the bottom.

Finally take a piece of red ribbon and bind the two sides of the bag to cover the rough edges.

You are now ready to perform.

Show the red bag, take out the knitting and shake out the beans or beads. Put your hand into the black part and turn the bag inside out to show the black lining.

Each time you want to change the colour of the bag you put your hand into the colour you want and reverse the bag. To show that it has a black lining every time you simply turn it inside out with your hand in the black part.

Always keep the mouth of the bag pointing away from the audience, and bring it round as you turn the bag inside out. The black bound edges of the bag will prevent anyone catching a glimpse of the hidden colours.

When you come to the part of the story where the bag turns striped, you simply turn it with the striped part out. And to show that the lining is now white, you simply turn it inside out with your hand in the white part.

Practise carefully this turning inside out. You must get used to finding the colour you want with a quick downward glance. Don't let it look as if you were hunting for one particular peanut in a bagful.

To make this trick really mysterious, it is a good idea to do another trick with the bag before you do the colour changing part. In this trick you give the bag to someone to hold, and you can be sure they'll have a good look at it. But of course the bag you give him is not the special trick bag but an ordinary red bag with a black lining, the same size as the trick one. Then you secretly change this ordinary bag for the special one and go on to the colour changing trick.

I'll show you how to manage this.

Suppose you use the bag first for the trick 'Eyes in your finger tips'. It is very suitable for this and you can let someone in the audience hold the bag while you do the trick.

At the end of this card trick you put the pack of cards into your Handy Box, pick up the box and lay the bag on the table. Then you put the box somewhere else out of the way.

Now, unknown to the audience, the trick bag is lying on the table under the Handy Box. There is a space under the box that lets you do this. You hold the plain bag in your right hand and the pack of cards in your left. Put the cards into the box and pick up the box with the same hand. Lift the box by the back edge and tilt it forward a little without lifting it off the table. With your right hand put the bag under the box, then lift the box with both hands, keeping the bag concealed under the box and revealing the trick bag on the table.

To the audience it looks as if you had just picked up the box and put the bag on the table.

You can now go on to the story of Aunt Jane losing her bag and the colour changing bag trick. As someone in the audience has already had a good look at the bag which everyone thinks is the one you are now using, the colour changes will come as a big surprise.

While we are talking about colour-changing tricks, here is another one that you can do.

The handkerchief changes colour

Of course you won't do this trick immediately after Aunt Jane's bag. In fact it will be better not to do it in the same programme as the bag because the effect is rather too much the same.

You show a handkerchief, say a blue one, and by drawing it through your hand you change its colour to orange. If you like you can have a handkerchief with a pattern on it and make the colours of the pattern change but the pattern remains the same. For instance a handkerchief with red roses on a yellow background could change to yellow roses on a blue background. But that depends on what kind of patterned material you can get.

How to do it

To make the special handkerchief you need two pieces of thin but opaque material about fifteen to eighteen inches square. Silk is best if you can get it. One piece is blue and one orange, or any other two quite different colours you like.

Lay the two pieces of material exactly on top of each other

74

and sew them together with a stitch or two right in the very middle.

Now fold the handkerchiefs in half diagonally as shown in Figure 25. Sew them together along the outer edges from A to B, but leave a space unsewn for an inch or so at corner A.

Next you want a metal curtain ring. This must be just big enough to pull the double handkerchief through easily. Sew this ring into corner A. To do this, cut the corner off, tuck the cut edges down and sew the ring between them to make a neat finish.

Now take corner C of the inner handkerchief and pass it up, inside the double handkerchief and out through the ring so that just the tip projects. Figure 26.

You now have a handkerchief that you can hold up by the ring corner and show quite freely. It looks like an

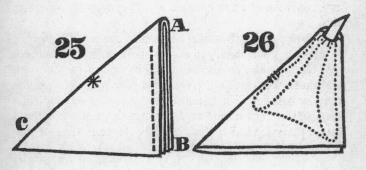

ordinary handkerchief. When you draw it through your hand you hold the ring with your left hand and pull the projecting corner through with your right hand. The handkerchief will turn inside out and so change colour.

As this is just a quick little trick, you can use it as a sort of magical incident. For instance you can take the hand-kerchief out of your pocket, wipe your hands with it, change its colour and put it back in your pocket. Do this quite casually without making any reference to it. A little surprise like this adds a great deal to the magical atmosphere of a performance.

You will of course see by now that another little piece of magic is needed to get all this sewing done. The secret is to get on the right side of Mum by helping to dry up the dishes after dinner. Or you might get your sister if you have one (but not if you haven't of course) or an obliging girl friend, to do the sewing for you. On the other hand if you, who are reading this, happen to be a lady girl you'll know how to do the job anyway. One very good solution to this business of getting sewing done for magical purposes will be found in Group Magic.

The magic chalk

You begin this trick by showing a white chalk which you say has magical properties. It can write any colour you like.

To prove this you pick up a slate, show it both sides, and ask the audience to call out the names of colours. As they do so you write the names of the colours on the slate, i.e., red, blue, yellow, and so on.

'You see, my magic chalk writes any colour,' you say. 'But perhaps that isn't what you thought I meant.' You turn the slate with the written side away from the audience and put the chalk on the table. 'Perhaps you expected my magic chalk to write actually in different colours. Well I won't disappoint you, because that is exactly what it has done.'

You turn the slate round and the audience see that all the names of the colours are now written in their own colours, red is in red chalk, blue in blue chalk and so on. You give the slate to someone in the audience, together with a damp cloth, and ask them to be good enough to clean the slate for you. That's a better way of proving that the slate is ordinary than asking them to examine it.

How to do it

The slate really is an ordinary one. But the best kind of slate to use isn't really a slate. So get, if you can, one of those sort of un-slates made of black cardboard in a wooden frame. You then need a piece of black cardboard cut to fit snugly inside the frame, forming a sort of loose flap on top of the slate. If you can't get black cardboard, use a piece of thin white card and paint it black on one side. Cover the other side of this flap with newspaper, pasted on. Figure 27.

On one side of the slate – we'll call it a slate even though it's made of cardboard – write the names of several colours, using chalk of the appropriate colour. You will want to remember the order in which you have written these colours. A good way to do this is to write first, across the top of the slate, the three primary colours, red, yellow, blue. Then under them you write the three secondary colours, green, orange, purple. Finally at the bottom of the slate you can write brown and grey, two of the tertiary colours. You don't need white, but that is'nt really a colour, and black, of course, wouldn't show on your black slate.

Now cover the coloured writing by laying over it the

prepared piece of cardboard, black side out. You can then show the slate to be black on both sides, by keeping the flap in position with your fingers.

On your table you have one or two sheets of newspaper and a white chalk. It is a good idea to doll up this white chalk a bit by fitting it into a cardboard tube and having some curly wires hanging from it. In fact the more attention you can draw to the chalk the better. Lead the audience to think the chalk is a special one and they aren't so likely to think there's anything special about the slate.

Having shown the chalk and talked about its magic qualities, pick up the slate, show both sides of it and hold it with the flap side towards the audience. Ask for the names of colours and as they are called out write them on the flap in about the same positions as you know you have written them in colour on the slate. You're sure to have the usual colours, red, green, yellow, and so on called out, and even if all the colours you want are not called out, you can still write them all down. Naturally you take no notice if someone calls out a fancy colour like moonlight blue or exploded strawberry pink.

Now turn the slate round with the writing away from the audience. As you say, 'Perhaps you expected my magic chalk to write actually in different colours,' you rest the slate on the table for a moment and let the flap fall off on the newspapers. It will be quite invisible there as the back of it is covered with newspaper.

Then as you say, 'Well, I won't disappoint you, because that is exactly what it has done,' you bring the slate forward, away from the table, then turn it round so that the coloured writing can be seen.

By the way, if your writing is as frightful as mine, you'd better print the names of the colours in capital letters. The trick would be rather a collapsible flop if nobody could read what you had written.

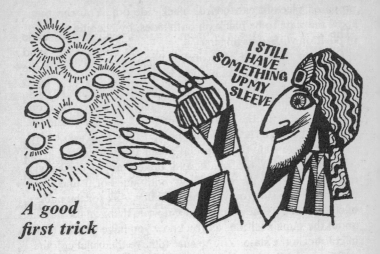

I STILL HAVE SOMETHING UP MY SLEEVE

A good first trick

I don't mean this is a good first trick to learn, but a good trick to start a show with.

You come on with a purse in your hand. 'I always think a good way to start any kind of show is to give money away,' you say. You open the purse and take out what appear to be some gold and silver coins, and throw them out to the audience. Actually they are chocolate coins covered with gold and silver paper. You can buy them at most sweet-shops.

Having thrown out the coins, you then calmly take your magic wand out of the purse. This is a wooden rod about fifteen inches long and couldn't possibly have got into the purse, so this makes quite an astonishing piece of magic.

Naturally the audience will think the wand folds up in some way. So you drop it, bonk, on the floor, then give it to someone to hold while you get ready for the next trick. He'll have a good look at it and discover that it is an ordinary piece of wooden rod and doesn't fold up or collapse at all.

How to do it

The purse is an ordinary one and you can probably persuade Mum to give you an old one of hers. It must be the kind that closes at the top with a clip sort of fastener, not the kind with a flap. You must now cut a short slit in the bottom of the purse. If there is a seam across the bottom, which there probably will be in this kind of purse, you can just undo a few stitches and open the seam. Figure 28.

The wand is just what I said it was. A wooden rod about half an inch in diameter and fifteen inches long. You should paint it black with white ends. Or you can cover it with shiny black paper and stick white paper round the ends.

The chocolate coins are also ordinary, but if you find

them a bit expensive, you can use instead a few toffees. In that case you don't say you're going to give money away but simply say 'give something away'.

To prepare for the trick, slide the wand up your left sleeve until the end of it comes just in the middle of the palm of your hand. You may find fifteen inches is too long for the wand, in which case you will have to make it a little shorter. Try it out with the piece of wooden rod and get it the right length before you paint it. With the wand in your sleeve you should be able to hold your arm bent and your hand in front of you without the other end of the wand pushing your coat sleeve out.

Now put your toffees or chocolate coins into the purse.

81

Close the purse and hold it in your hand and push the end of the wand just through the slit in the bottom of the purse.

You now walk forward, open the purse, throw out the sweets, then very deliberately draw out the wand through the slit in the bottom of the purse. It will look exactly as if it came out of the purse. Figure 29.

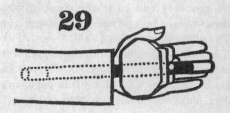

Drop the wand on the floor and at the same time slip the purse into your jacket pocket. Nobody is likely to ask to see the purse because you go straight on to the next trick. However, if you want to be very professional, and if you're going to lash out and actually buy a purse for this trick, you could buy two purses exactly alike. Then you prepare one for the trick and have the other one in your left jacket pocket. After the trick, when you have put the prepared purse in your pocket, you can take out the ordinary purse, which the audience will think is the one you have just used, and hand it to someone, asking him to see if there are any more magic wands left in it. In this way you convince the audience that the purse is ordinary and the wand not collapsible and they're left with no possible solution to the mystery.

Confetti squash

There is a box containing confetti on your table. You pick up a handful and let it trickle back into the box to show that it is confetti. Then you fill a goblet with it, heaping it full to overflowing.

'People use funny things to make drinks with nowadays,' you say, 'but I don't expect you've ever heard of anyone making a drink out of confetti.'

You throw a handkerchief over the goblet of confetti.

'I've found it makes a very nice drink, if you make it the right way,' you continue. You then take the handkerchief off the goblet, pick up a glass and pour lemonade or some other drink out of the goblet into the glass. The confetti has apparently changed to lemonade.

'There you are,' you say, 'Confetti Squash. Very refreshing. Try some.' You hand the glass to someone in the audience to drink.

How to do it

The box of confetti is quite ordinary. It is just a cardboard box about fifteen inches long and eight inches wide. The height of the box must be an inch or two more than the height of the goblet you are going to use. Cover the box with fancy paper of course.

You want two goblets exactly alike. Those nice coloured aluminium goblets are just the thing, but if you can't get them you could use two waxed cardboard picnic goblets. You also want a thing that conjurers call a fake. In this case the fake is a little patty tin the right size to fit on top of one of the goblets, and so form a sort of very shallow lining. Figure 30. To this patty tin fix a short loop of thin wire. Do

30

this by punching two tiny holes in the edge of the patty tin and twisting the ends of the wire through them. Now stick confetti all over the inside of the patty tin.

To prepare the trick, pour lemonade or some other cold drink into one of the goblets. Put the patty tin on the goblet and fill the patty tin with confetti. Put the goblet into the box near the left hand, as you stand beside the box, and at the front of the box. Pour some confetti into the box and stand the second goblet on your table in front of the box.

First show the confetti by taking a handful out and letting it trickle back. Pick up the goblet and rattle your wand, or perhaps a spoon inside and let everyone see that the goblet is empty. 'I've had this goblet a long time,' you might say, 'ever since it was an egg cup.'

Now dip the goblet into the box and scoop confetti into it. Do this by holding the goblet in your right hand and using your left hand to push the confetti in. Bring out the goblet and pour the confetti back into the box, saying, 'There are forty-eight million confets in this confetti. I'll let you count them later on.'

Now you apparently scoop the goblet full of confetti again. But this time you leave the goblet in the box and bring out the one with the lemonade in. The patty tin of confetti on top of this goblet makes it look as if it were full of confetti.

Blow all the loose confetti off the top and throw a handkerchief over the goblet. When you take the handkerchief off you grip the wire loop through the handkerchief and so lift off the patty tin as well. Drop the handkerchief and patty tin into the confetti box, pick up a glass tumbler and pour out the lemonade.

Blowing the confetti off the top of the goblet makes a delightful mess on the floor. So I suggest that for this trick you spread a large cloth of some kind on the floor before you start. You can explain that it is a magic carpet to help the trick. Really of course it's to save Mum from blowing her top when she sees confetti all over her lovely drawing room. This is called psychology.

Of course you can do the show in the garage and sweep the mess up afterwards.

It's well worth taking a little trouble to make a nice job of this trick, both as regards making the things and as regards learning to do the secret exchange neatly. Because it gives you the means of doing a whole lot of different tricks.

For instance, instead of changing the confetti into lemonade you can turn it into coloured ribbons, or into a little doll, or into sweets. Or instead of confetti you can use bran, say it is sawdust, and change it into a block of wood. Or you can use confetti and change it into rice. I'm sure you'll enjoy thinking your brains out straight inventing different effects to produce with this trick.

Magic flowers
a Professor Branestawm sort of trick

This is a lovely showy trick and a sure applause winner.
There is quite a bit of making to do to construct the special
things needed, but it is the kind of making you learn in the
way of handicrafts at school (I hope) and it's very good fun.

The effect of the trick is as follows.

You have a large sort of portfolio, consisting of two
pieces of cardboard hinged with cloth. You open it and take
out several pictures of flowers. The portfolio contains nothing else.

You put the pictures back and close the portfolio. Then
you pick up one of those scent sprays that has a rubber bulb
on it. You squeeze the bulb and the scent comes out in a fine
spray. You needn't use Mum's Chanel Number 5, ordinary
water will do. If you can't get hold of a scent spray ask Mum
to let you have one of those aerosols containing anti-smell
stuff. You'll only use one puff for the trick.

'This is a special kind of stuff invented by Professor
Branestawm,' you explain. 'He called it Branestawm's Be-

wildering Bacteria, or The Secret of Life Revealed. It will bring to life any picture to which it is applied. At least that's what Professor Branestawm said. Let's see if it works.'

You puff a spray at the portfolio of flower pictures. Then you open the portfolio and take out several baskets of lovely flowers, all of them much too big to have been hidden in the flat portfolio.

How to do it

First I'll explain how to make the portfolio. For this you want three pieces of thick cardboard, each about fifteen inches by ten. Hinge two of them together by the long sides

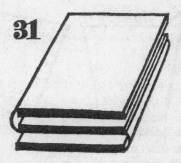

31

with a strip of thin cloth. Now hinge the remaining piece by one of its long sides to the long side of one of the hinged pieces. You now have a sort of double portfolio that can be opened either side. Figure 31. When you stick the hingeing cloth on, allow a bit of space between the edges of the pieces of cardboard so that when the portfolio is folded there is room for something thickish between the covers.

The baskets of flowers are made to fold flat. I'll show you how to make them in a minute. The folded flat baskets of flowers are put into one side of the portfolio and the pictures of flowers are put into the other side. You can cut the flower pictures from an old seed catalogue.

To perform the trick, open the portfolio at the side where the pictures are. Show the flower pictures and let everyone see there is nothing else in the portfolio. Put the pictures back and close the portfolio. As you turn to put it on your table, you turn the portfolio right over so that the part with the folded baskets inside is on top.

Pick up the spray, tell the story of Professor Branestawm's wonderful invention and puff a spray at the portfolio. Pick up the portfolio, open it with the opening away from the audience and take out the baskets of flowers, arranging them on the table.

Now, how to make the folding baskets of flowers.

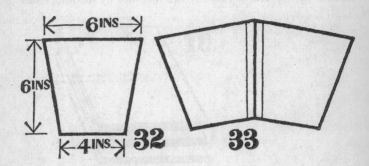

Begin by cutting four pieces of thin but stiff card to the shape shown in Figure 32. Lay two of these close together on the table and hinge them together with sticky tape as shown in Figure 33. Hinge two more pieces together in the same way.

Now lay these double hinged pieces exactly on top of each other. Hinge them together at the outer edges with tape. You must do this by laying the tape along with just over half the width of the tape projecting over the edge, then fold this part under and smooth it down. You now have a sort of tapering box with no top or bottom. It can be folded flat. Figure 34 shows an end view of how it folds.

The next thing to do is to cover this folding box with fancy paper. You can get fancy paper printed to look like basketwork and that is what you use. If you can get some of the self-adhesive plastic, which is also made with a basket pattern, it will make a stronger job. But the plastic is rather expensive so you may have to make do with the paper.

Now make a small slit through the taped fold on the two sides I have marked A and B in Figure 34, that is the diagonally opposite sides of the box, the sides that fold, not the sides that go flat.

Take an elastic band and poke one end through the slit from inside and push a matchstick through the loop on the

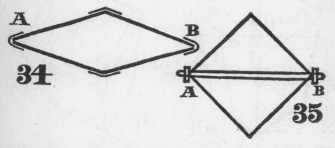

outside of the box. Stretch the elastic, push the other end through the slit on the other side of the box and fix that by pushing a matchstick through on the outside of the box. Figure 35.

The exact size and strength of elastic band you will have to find by experiment. The ones I use for boxes of this size are four and a half inches long and three-sixteenths of an inch wide.

You will now find that if you squash the box flat and let go it will spring into shape again.

You will also find that the elastic bands may tend to pull the box a little out of the square. So you fix a piece of string between the other diagonally opposite corners. The string crosses the elastic band and is fixed by matchsticks in the same way. This string stops the box from opening too far. Figure 36. Stick little bits of the basket paper over the matchsticks to hide them.

Now you want a piece of card five and three quarter inches square. Cut it in two, diagonally, and hinge these two pieces together with tape so that they can fold.

This folding piece must now be hinged with tape to two sides of the folding box. Now be careful about this. Look at Figure 37 which is a looking down view on top of the box.

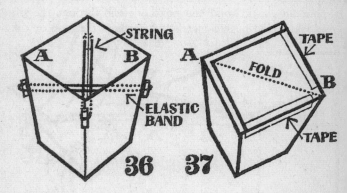

The square folding piece is tape-hinged by two adjacent sides to the top of the box. The fold in the cardboard square runs diagonally across the box. And it is hinged to the box so that the elastic band in the box goes the same way as the fold in the square.

If you have done this properly you will now be able to fold the box flat and, when you let go of it, it will spring back into a square box. I call it a box but now of course it looks like a basket owing to the basket pattern paper you have covered it with.

Now to make the flowers.

You want some dark green tissue paper for leaves and some bright coloured tissue paper for the flowers.

To make a flower cut a piece of tissue paper about

five inches square. Fold it diagonally and crease the fold well.

Now open it out flat and turn it over.

Fold it in halves straight across. Open it and fold it straight across the opposite way.

Notice that in these last two folds the paper is folded the opposite way to the diagonal fold. Figure 38.

Now fold the paper by tucking the diagonal folds inwards. You will then find you have a folded piece of tissue paper that looks like Figure 39.

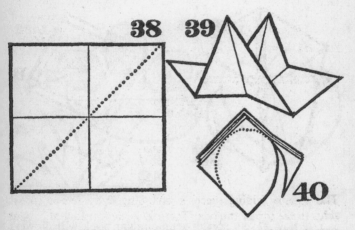

Trim the edges that are not folded, as in Figure 40, to a sort of petal shape.

You now have a little folding paper flower.

Next cut two pieces of green tissue to the same shape as the flower. It is a good idea to cut a piece of card to this size and shape and draw round it on the tissue to get the same shape every time.

Stick one of these leaves to each side of the flower, sticking the paper only at the bottom.

You want nine of these flowers for each basket.

This is how you mount them in the basket.

Cut two circles of thin but stiffish green paper eight inches in diameter and fold each in halves.

Stick the two discs together along the folded edges so that they open like the leaves of a book. Figure 41.

Now stick three flowers in a row inside each of these three folds. Figure 42 shows you how to stick the flowers in. Stick each flower to the top edge of the paper disc and stick only just the top of the flower. Each flower is stuck at each side between the leaves formed by the paper discs. Figure 43 shows a sectional view of how the flowers are stuck in.

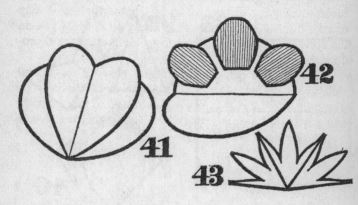

You now have a sort of semi-circular book with flowers stuck between the leaves. When the book is opened out flat the flowers open too.

Open out this sort of book of flowers and stick it to the hinged square in the top of the flower basket. See that the folded edges of the flower book run along the folded edge of the top of the flower basket.

Now you have what looks like a basket of flowers. You can fold it flat but when you let go of it, it will spring into shape.

Make several of these baskets, some with red flowers, some with yellow, and perhaps one or two with mixed colour flowers. You will find that you can comfortably get four of these folded baskets into your portfolio.

To prepare the trick, fold the baskets and put them into one side of the portfolio. Close the portfolio. You will find that the flower baskets will expand and push the portfolio open again, so you must either have a little clip to keep the portfolio closed or else put something heavy on it to keep it flat on the table.

When showing the trick, pick up the portfolio and hold it so that the baskets don't push it open. Open the side with the pictures in and show them. Close it and put it on the table, turning it over as you do so. If you don't use a clip to keep it closed, put something heavy on it while you do the spraying business. Then pick up the portfolio and produce the baskets, one at a time.

This is a very effective and showy piece of magic and well worth the time it will take you to make the baskets. They are not difficult to make if you do the job carefully and neatly, one step at a time, and follow the directions I have given you.

The escaping handkerchief

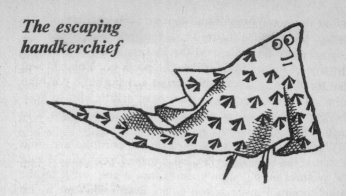

By the time you've made all those folding flower baskets you'll begin to think making magic is worse than being at school. So now let's try something that doesn't need so much hard work.

You have a tumbler and a little silk handkerchief. You pour water into the tumbler and either drink it or pour it back into the jug. Dry the tumbler and put the silk handkerchief inside. Then you cover the tumbler with a cloth and put an elastic band round it, rather like putting the cover on a pot of jam.

'The handkerchief is now held a prisoner in the crystal castle,' you say. You ask someone to hold the covered tumbler and act as warder of the prison.

'You wouldn't make a very good warder you know,' you remark, 'because your prisoner has escaped.'

You put your hand under the cloth and draw out the silk handkerchief. When the cloth is taken off the tumbler is seen to be empty.

How to do it

You need one of those clear plastic tumblers. You then make a hole in the side of it, about an inch from the bottom. The hole must be about three-quarters of an inch in diameter, big enough to draw the silk handkerchief through easily, but small enough for you to hold your thumb over. Figure 44. The best way to make the hole is to get Dad to drill a hole and gradually enlarge it to the right size. Be careful not to split the plastic. Smooth the edges of the hole with a bit of fine glasspaper.

You will now find that if you hold the tumbler with your thumb pressed firmly on the hole, you can pour water into the tumbler and it won't leak out.

To perform the trick, bring the tumbler forward and pour

44

water into it from a jug, pressing your thumb over the hole to keep the water in. Drink the water, or pour it back into the jug, according to whether you're thirsty, or like neat water, or not.

Dry the tumbler and tuck the little silk handkerchief into it. As you do this arrange to get one corner of the handkerchief poked a teeny bit through the hole and grip it on the outside of the tumbler with your thumb.

Throw the cloth over the tumbler and snap the elastic band round. You can now let someone hold the covered glass. Show your hands empty, reach under the cloth and draw the silk handkerchief out through the hole.

Remove the elastic band and uncover the tumbler showing that the silk handkerchief really has escaped.

It is a good idea to finish the trick by pouring water in and out of the tumbler as before, to convince everybody that it is an ordinary tumbler.

A Chinese sort of story

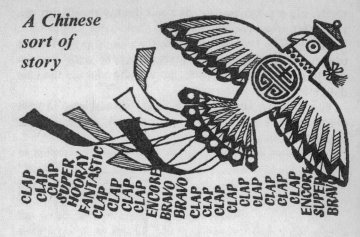

CLAP CLAP CLAP SUPER HOORAY FANTASTIC CLAP CLAP CLAP CLAP ENCORE BRAVO BRAVO CLAP CLAP CLAP CLAP CLAP CLAP CLAP CLAP CLAP ENCORE SUPER BRAVO

On your stage, or in that part of the room you are using as a stage, you have an assistant who is holding a fancy shaped board from which hang six Chinese banners painted in various colours. It will dress up the trick very nicely if your assistant is wearing a Chinese jacket and is made up a bit to look Chinese. You also have a Chinese looking box with a lid.

You begin the trick by showing the box empty. The best way to do this is to tip it upside down and let something fall out. Don't say anything about the box being empty, just tip the box over then stand it right way up again. The thing you tip out of the box is a Chinese hat. One of those paper and cardboard affairs you can buy at shops that sell party novelties.

You put the hat on and start talking.

'In a street in the town of Fu T'Yu,' you say, 'there were a number of shopkeepers who wanted to have a day off each week to go to the dragon races. But none of them would shut his shop while the others remained open in case they pinched his honourable customers. So they decided to meet at the town hall to discuss the matter.'

You take the first banner off its hook and roll it up. 'First came Hi Pong, the fishmonger. He wanted to close on Monday because his week-end holiday made him so tired he didn't want to work on Monday.'

You drop the rolled-up banner into the box and take the next banner, rolling that up and dropping it into the box with the first one.

'Then came Sho Mee Shu the shoemaker. He wanted to close on Tuesday because his girl friend had Tuesdays off.'

You continue taking the banners, rolling them up and dropping them into the box.

'Sum Bunz the baker preferred to have Wednesday off because that was the day his wife did the washing in their flat over the shop and he liked to be a long way off.'

'Thursday was the choice of Li Chepe the letter writer because the post went on Wednesday. Chop Tu the butcher wanted to close on Friday because that was the day his assistant had to be paid and he thought it would be cheaper to be out.'

'And finally Un Yun the greengrocer wanted closing day to be Saturday because he didn't see why he should agree with any of the others.'

You pick up the box with the rolled-up banners in it, move your table forward and put the box on it.

'There was then a considerable amount of oriental argument in the town hall. But on the third day of the seventh week, after the five hundred and ninth bowl of tea, all the shopkeepers hit on a wonderful solution of their problem. They all agreed to close for half a day every day and start work the middle of the night before to make up for it. So the conference ended and the shopkeepers went back to their shops.'

You clap your hands and all the six banners appear hanging from the fancy board once more.

'And the Chinese dove of peace rose mystically over the town hall.'

You take from the box a comic looking sort of parrot with a pigtail and wearing a Chinese hat.

How to do it

The six Chinese banners can be made from paper. Don't use cartridge paper, it's too stiff. What you want is some fairly thin, soft paper. Your local arts and crafts shop will probably have something suitable. Or you could use those fancy papers sold for wrapping up presents. Choose papers with very subdued designs so that the Chinese lettering you paint on the paper will show up.

If you want the banners to last a long time, it will be better to make them from some kind of fabric. A cheap thin satin is good and can be had in many bright colours. You can draw the Chinese lettering on the satin with those felt tipped marking things that are like a little sort of bottle of special ink with a felt nib.

Each banner measures about six inches wide by two feet long. You stick a thin wooden rod across each end, letting the rod project about an inch at each side. To the top rod tie a piece of string to make a loop to hang the banner up.

Figure 45 shows you the correct Chinese designs you can use for the various shopkeepers, so copy them carefully. Use different coloured papers for the different banners and different colours for the Chinese signs. Blue signs on yellow paper for one, black signs on red paper for another, red on white for another and so on.

You will want two of each banner. The second set of banners is prepared a little differently from the other. Instead of putting a short rod into the top and bottom of each banner, you have a long thin wooden rod going along the tops of all six banners. The banners are fixed to the rod with spaces between the banners. The bottoms of the ban-

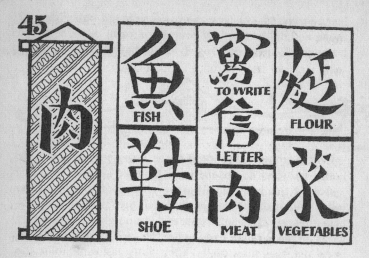

Figure 45

FISH

TO WRITE LETTER

FLOUR

SHOE

MEAT

VEGETABLES

ners are similarly fixed to a rod but this must be a heavy rod. A length of metal curtain rod is about right. See Figure 46.

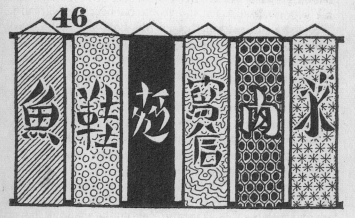

Figure 46

The fancy board must be nearly four feet long, to make room for all the banners to hang from it. You cut it from a piece of plywood with a fretsaw and you can make it as fancy as you like or have the patience to cut out. Figure 47 shows a simple design. Of course you paint one side of the board in a Chinese-looking style, as I have shown.

On the front of this board at the lower edge are six little hooks on which the banners are hung.

Behind this board is a narrow shelf running almost the full length of the board. On this shelf the six duplicate banners are laid. The banners are rolled up tight and the string loops on the tops are fixed under the shelf.

At the beginning of the trick your assistant holds the board up high with the six banners hung on the hooks. He keeps the six hidden banners from rolling off the shelf by holding the ends of the rolled banners with his thumbs.

When you have taken the visible banners off the board, rolled them up and put them in the box, you make them reappear on the board by clapping your hands. Your assistant then releases the hidden banners and tilts the board back a little, when the six duplicate banners will drop off and unroll, appearing in position hanging from the board.

Of course you must take care to arrange the hidden banners in the same order as the visible ones.

You may be lucky enough to get Mum to lend you a Chinese jacket, if she has one, but just in case, here are instructions for making one. See Figure 48. Cut out the shape shown on the left, from some Chinese-looking material. The best way is to fold the material in half inside-out, and with the fold at the top, cut out the shape as shown on the right. Sew up the sides and along under the arms. Hem the bottom edge and the front openings, cuffs, and collar. The circular Chinese design on the front of the

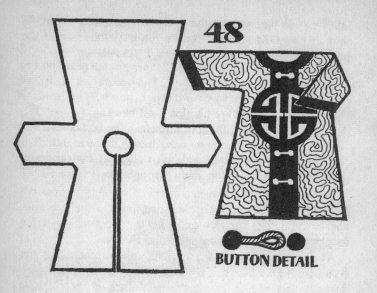

48

BUTTON DETAIL

jacket is easily made by cutting the sign out of felt and sewing it to a disc of contrasting coloured felt, then cut it in halves down the middle and sew one half to each side of the jacket.

Now for the town hall box.

This is quite easy to make from fairly thick cardboard. It should be about eighteen inches high, eight inches wide and eight inches long. In other words it is a square box eighteen inches high. There is no bottom to the box. Or rather the bottom is fixed twelve inches from one end. So the box is divided into two compartments, one twelve inches deep and one six inches deep. There is a lid on each end. You make these lids from pieces of cardboard six inches square and you glue two pieces of thick wood under each square so that the lids fit, one on each end of the box. You must make them a fairly tight fit so that they will not fall off when the box is turned over. Each lid has a small hole in the centre so that you can put a finger through the hole to take the lid off. Figure 49 shows the whole thing.

You now decorate the box with fancy paper with a fairly small design and stick coloured tapes round near the top, in the middle and at the bottom. The decoration must look the same whichever way up the box stands. The inside of the box and the lids are painted dead black.

There is one more thing to do before the box is ready for use. You fix a handle on one side, exactly in the middle. This handle can be a piece of wide tape glued at each end with enough slack to get your hand through. See Figure 50.

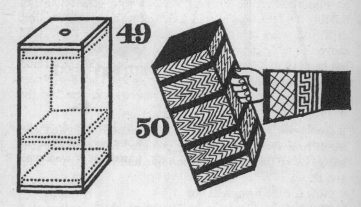

Finally you will need the Chinese dove of peace. In making this you can let yourself go and make the most unlikely looking bird you can think of. An easy way to make it is to cut it out of coloured felt, cutting two bird shaped pieces and sewing them together with a little cotton wool put in loosely for stuffing. Sew on some feathers and coloured ribbons and finally fix a string to the bird's neck for lifting him out. Jill McDonald has drawn you a lovely Chinese dove of peace to inspire you.

The working of the trick will now be almost as clear as a glass of water in a dark cupboard.

You put the dove of peace into the shallow side of the box, put on the lid and turn the box over. Put the Chinese hat into the deep side of the box and stand the box on a small table to your right.

At your left and a bit farther back stands your assistant holding the board with the banners.

First take the lid off the box, tip the Chinese hat out and put it on.

As you refer to each banner, take it off the board, roll it up and drop it into the box. When all the banners are in the box put the lid on and push it down tight. Now comes an important move. Pick up the box with your left hand, holding it by the tape handle. Let the box hang by your side, as if you were carrying a suitcase. With your right hand move the table forward a little. As you do this, turn your left hand so that the box swings round, then when you stand it on the table it will be the other way up. This is quite an easy move but don't forget to practise it until you find the way that suits you best.

Now clap your hands, your assistant lets the duplicate banners drop, you take the lid off the box and produce the Chinese dove of peace to, let's hope, tornadoes of applause.

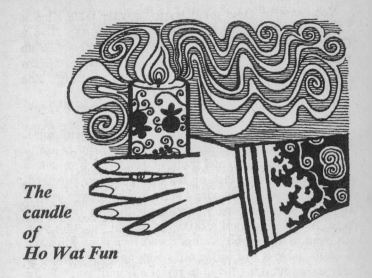

The candle of Ho Wat Fun

This is another trick with a Chinese setting, but quite different from the one about the shopkeepers of Fu T'Yu.

You have on your table a Chinese-looking candle in a candlestick. You may be able to get a candle with a willow pattern on it or even a fancy candle with dragons on, but these may be a bit expensive. You can make your own Chinese candle quite easily by covering a piece of wooden rod with white paper and painting a dragon or some other Chinese design on it. Let the paper covering stick out about an inch beyond the wooden rod and put a piece of real candle in the space. The candle has nothing to do with the working of the trick but it is important because of the little story woven round it.

'This is the magic candle of Ho Wat Fun, the wonderful wizard of Wun Tu,' you say. 'The remarkable thing about it is that while it is alight you can't believe your eyes. Let me show you.'

104

You point to three small boxes on your table. One is black, one white and one green, and each can have a Chinese sign on it to indicate the contents. You pick up the black box and tip out of it a little black bag and show that the bag contains tea, the dry sort, not a cup of tea. You put the bag of tea back into the black box.

Now you show, in the same way, that the white box contains a bag of rice and the green one contains a bag with a piece of green silk in it.

'I shall now light the mysterious candle of Ho Wat Fun,' you say. You strike a match and light the candle.

'Now watch,' you continue. 'I take the three bags out of their boxes. I put the bag of rice from the white box into the green box. The bag of tea from the black box goes into the white box and the bag of green silk from the green box goes into the black box.'

As you say these words you show each bag and its contents and put the bags into different boxes from those they came from.

'The white rice is now not in the white box, the black tea has been taken from the black box and the green silk isn't in the green box,' you say. 'That's what you think. But as I told you; while the mystic candle of Ho Wat Fun is alight you can't believe your eyes.'

You blow out the candle. A nice way to do this is by waving a fan in front of it.

'The black tea has never left the black box.' You take the bag out of the black box and pour tea from it. 'The white rice has been in the white box all the time.' You pour rice from the bag taken from the white box. 'And the green box still contains the green silk.' You take out the bag and draw out the green silk.

How to do it

The candle has nothing to do with the working of the trick as I have said. The secret is all in the three boxes. Each box is made in the same way.

Make the boxes from stiff cardboard. Each one should measure about five inches by five inches and be seven inches deep. There is nothing special about the boxes but you must fit each with a hinged partition, as shown in Figure 51. The easiest way to fit this partition is to cut a square of cardboard slightly less than five inches square to fit easily into the box and lie snugly on the bottom. Now cut a piece

TEA   RICE   SILK

of cardboard slightly less than five inches wide and six and a half inches long. Hinge this with sticky tape across the centre of the five inch square. If you put this thing into the box you will find you have a partition that can be swung from side to side in the box, dividing the box into two compartments.

Paint the insides of the boxes and all sides of the partitions black and decorate the outside of the boxes with Chinese signs meaning rice, tea and silk. See Figure 52.

You now want six little black bags. These should be made of thin material. Each should be quite small, so that when it is filled with rice or tea it can be concealed under the swinging flap of one of the boxes.

106

To prepare the trick, fill two bags with rice, two with tea and tuck a piece of green silk into each of the other two. Put the two bags of tea into the black box, one each side of the partition. Put the two bags of rice one each side of the partition in the white box and the two bags of green silk one each side of the partition in the green box.

You will now see that when you take the bags out of the boxes and put them into boxes of different colours, you can show that they are really in the boxes they came from simply by taking out the bags from the other sides of the partitions.

The reason for using the black bags to hold the rice, tea and silk is that if you put these things into the boxes loose they would leak through the partitions and give the trick away.

Tew Tewbes

The spelling is awful but the magic is good. You have two tubes about ten inches long. One is four inches in diameter and the other is a little larger, so that one will go inside the other. Cardboard postal tubes will be fine, but you will of course, cover them with fancy paper, or paint them some very high class colours.

You show the tubes to be empty and stand them on your table, one inside the other. You then fix tissue paper over each end of the nested tubes, with elastic bands. Then you break the paper at one end and produce a number of silk scarves. Finally from the silk scarves you produce either a tremendously enormous great flag or else a big basket of flowers.

This is a very good piece of magic to finish a show because it makes a big colourful display.

How to do it

The outer tube of the two is just a cardboard tube with nothing special about it. The inner one is considerably crafty. To make it you want another tube, an inch in diameter and a little shorter than the big tube. Fasten the narrow tube inside the big one with glue or sticky tape, so that it lies along one side, as shown in Figure 53.

Now cut a circle of cardboard to fit snugly into the big tube. Out of this, at one edge, cut a circle to fit over the narrow tube. Figure 54. Stick this disc into the big tube, at one end of the narrow tube. Now pack your silk scarves into the space between the big and narrow tubes. Figure 55 gives you a sort of transparent view of what the whole thing looks like. The scarf at the open end should have some black

53

54

55

SILK-
SCARVES

OH-HO
VERY
CRAFTY
INDEED

on it and this black part should come on top. The insides of both tubes are painted black, so is the inside of the other big tube.

Have both the tubes standing on your table, one inside the other, with the open end of the inner tube upwards.

Lift off the outer tube, saying, 'Here are two tubes. One is a little bigger than the other. I managed that by having the other a little smaller than the one.'

Now pick up your magic wand. This can be the same one you used in the item called 'A Good First Trick'. It is just a wooden rod about half an inch thick and fifteen inches long, painted black with white ends. You put the wand through the tube and sort of spin the tube on it, letting the audience see through the tube as you do so. Let the tube slide off the wand on to the table. Next pick up the inner tube, slide your wand through the narrow tube inside the big one and spin this tube on the wand, but keep it sideways to the audience so that they can't see into it.

'These tubes are very easy to make. You just get a round piece of air and cover it with cardboard.'

Let the tube slide off the wand on to the table as before. Then pick up the empty tube and drop it over the loaded one.

Take a square of tissue paper and fit it over the outer tube with an elastic band. Turn the tubes over, but be enormously careful not to let the inner tube fall out. You needn't be afraid of doing this with noticeable care because the audience can see that you have to prevent the inner tube from falling out. Now put a piece of tissue paper over the other end of the tube with another elastic band, then turn the tubes the other way up again and hold them in your left hand.

While you are doing this you can say, 'One awkward thing about tubes is that although they have tops and bottoms, they don't have tops and bottoms. I'm sure that will be clear to intelligent people like you. So I make paper tops and bottoms to the tubes with these pieces of tissue paper and these elastic bands. It's rather like making a sort of drum. You can't get much music out of a drum like this, but you can get other things.'

As you say this, you break the paper at the top end of the tube and start drawing out the scarves. As you draw out each scarf you hold it against the tube with the fingers of the left hand that is holding the tube. When you have produced three or four scarves you go over to a table on your right. On this table is your Handy Box and under the false bottom of this is the large flag, folded up. Take the scarves in your right hand, and hold them up in front of the box. Your assistant takes the box away and you lay the scarves over the folded flag which is left behind on the table.

You produce the rest of the scarves, laying them on the first ones. Put the tubes aside, pick up the scarves and the flag with them. Then produce the flag.

You may not find this last bit very easy unless I tell you a good way to do it.

Prepare the flag by sewing a curtain ring to each of the top corners. Lay the flag on a table and fold it in pleats, starting at the bottom. Now fold the pleated strips in pleats. Press the parcel nice and flat and, if you like, put a strip of tissue paper round it and fasten the ends of the paper with sticky tape. This will keep everything secure.

When you pick up the flag with the scarves, get hold of the two rings, then bring your hands apart and let the scarves drop. As they fall to the floor the flag opens out, making a very effective display.

If you are going to produce a basket of flowers instead of the flag, you use one of the special baskets described in 'Magic Flowers'. This basket, folded flat, is concealed under the Handy Box in the same way as the flag, but with a little clip on it to keep it flat. You scoop up the scarves in a bundle, picking up the folded basket with them. Remove the clip and the basket will open and you take away the scarves to reveal it.

SPECIAL
MAGIC FOR
WEENY-WIZARDS
AND FUDDLE-
FINGERS

This section is particularly for little people hardly tall enough to see over the top of a rabbit. And for people who can't always get their fingers to do what they want them to. These tricks almost do themselves. It is very nearly impossible for them to go wrong, unless you make them go wrong, or are stupendously careless. As if you would be!

You might like to try some of these on your family, just to see what you can do, even though you thought you couldn't.

THIS ONE WILL REALLY FLUMMOX THEM!

Flying papers

You have six pieces of tissue paper, all different colours, or you can use six differently coloured paper napkins. 'I often wondered,' you say, 'how the chaps who deliver the newspapers in the morning manage to land them at the right houses. I've found out they do it by magic. Please imagine that these six coloured papers are newspapers. They're not unlike newspapers really, highly coloured and nothing in them.

'This one,' you show the green one, 'is the Green Gazette, it comes out whenever Wednesday falls on a Thursday. Here is the Blue Bulletin published every Bluesday. The Yellow Press, everybody's heard of that. The Pink Post and the White Weekly, which have blank pages for people who can't read, and finally The Friday Friend, which is orange coloured and is published specially for wrapping up fish and chips. Will somebody please choose one.'

Let us suppose somebody chooses the green piece.

'The Green Gazette, all right. Now we have to deliver the Green Gazette to Vase Villa, there it is on Mantelpiece Hill.' You point to a vase on the mantelpiece.

You then turn your trouser pocket inside out and back

again to show that it's empty. (Pick up any stray pocket money that falls out.) Then you tuck the green paper into the pocket.

'All I have to do is clap my hands. No bicycles to ride, no hurling the paper over the fence and hoping it doesn't land in the goldfish pond.' You clap your hands and turn the pocket inside out. The green paper has gone. Then you ask someone to look in the vase and there sure enough is the green paper.

How to do it

Of course you need two pieces of paper of each colour, but then you guessed that.

To make the chosen piece vanish from your pocket, you tuck it up into the top corner of your pocket as you push it in the pocket. You will then find you can turn the pocket inside out and the paper will remain hidden. It's so easy the cat could do it if he wore trousers.

The second piece of green paper is already in the vase waiting for someone to take it out when you tell them.

Yes, I know. Suppose someone chooses the pink piece or the blue piece or one of the others? You can't get out of that by writing the names of the colours on a little pad as the conjurer did in 'Wild Animals'. No, you get out of this an even easier way. You have a green piece in the vase, a pink piece hidden behind the clock, a blue piece in a drawer, and so on. All you have to do is remember where each different coloured paper is hidden. Then when one paper is chosen you simply announce that you will deliver that paper to Clock House or No. 2 Drawer Lane or wherever you know the other piece of that colour is hidden.

If you think you can't remember all that comic talk about the coloured papers, you can simply say you are going to make one of the papers fly across the room, then have one chosen and go on from there.

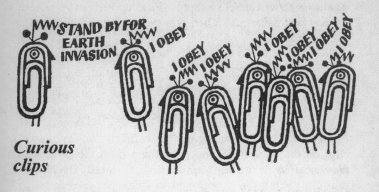

Curious clips

You show a number of those little wire clips that people use for fastening papers together.

'These are very useful,' you say, 'you can use them for all sorts of things, like clipping the pages of Mum's shopping list together so that they don't blow all over the Supermarket. Or you can use them as bookmarks.' You open a book and slip a clip on one of the pages.

'But there's rather a funny thing about these clips. I'll show you. Let's take half a dozen of them.' You count six clips on to the open book, then using the book as a tray, you pour the clips into a small basin.

'If you use these clips very much you keep finding you have more and more of them. I don't know where they come from. Perhaps it's from outer space. Look! Even in this little while they've gathered some of their friends.' You tip the clips out of the basin, count them out and there are now ten instead of six.

'I think we'd better stop now,' you say, 'or we shall have the room full of the things in no time.'

How to do it

If you open a book you will find there is a little sort of tunnel formed along the back, inside the binding. It isn't a big enough tunnel to get a train in but you can get a few paper clips in very easily. Put four clips in the tunnel and close the book. The back of the binding will then go flat and hold the clips in.

You show the six clips and use one as a bookmark just to give an excuse for using the book. Then you lay the six clips on the open book and pour them from the book into the basin. (Show the basin empty first). Naturally the hidden four clips will go in as well and so when you take the clips out of the basin there will be ten. You can have more than four clips in the binding if you like. It is just possible one might stick in the binding when you pour them into the basin, but it doesn't matter because you don't say how many there are going to be.

A thought-reading trick

This is a nice family trick. You ask the people in the room to think of some object in the room. 'You must all agree to think of the same thing,' you say. 'I'll go out of the room while you decide.'

You then tell them that your assistant will call you back when they have made up their minds what object they're going to think of.

When you are called back you say that with everyone thinking of the same thing the thoughts make so much noise you can hear them. Your assistant then goes round the room touching various things. When he touches the thing everybody has thought of you say, 'That's what you're all thinking of.' And you're right.

As a rule a conjurer should never repeat a trick, because if he does, the audience know what he is going to do and they are liable to guess how he does it. But this trick is different. You can do it several times, the people thinking of a different thing each time. You are able to say what object they're thinking of, and you are always right.

You must arrange this trick with the person who is going to be your assistant. He, of course, knows what object everybody has decided to think of. When you are called back into the room, your assistant is able to let you know what object has been thought of. He can do this in various ways and you arrange with him to do it in a different way each time, so that the audience is not able to guess the secret.

This is what you arrange with your assistant.

When you come back into the room after the first object has been thought of, your assistant touches various things in the room. He touches some particular thing, such as the clock, just before he touches the object thought of. So you know the next thing he touches after the clock is the one thought of.

Now you can't do the trick the same way next time otherwise people will soon guess that touching the clock is the secret. So for the second object thought of, you arrange for your assistant to touch this object, say fourth. Then you know what it is. If you want to do the trick yet again he can touch each object with his first finger, but touch the chosen object with his second finger. To do it yet again he can show you which is the chosen object by touching it sixth; that is to say he touches five things before touching the thought-of one.

This is a very effective piece of magic and it can't go wrong as long as you and your assistant remember what you have arranged. But don't do it too often. And you must tell the audience they must think of some actual thing in the room. No thinking of Uncle Joe's cold, or the Thank-You letter that Christopher wrote yesterday for a birthday present.

The vanishing penny

AHA! THE MAGIC IS TOO STRONG

You take a penny out of your pocket and put it in your left hand. Close your hand and ask someone in the audience to hold your wrist.

'I am now going to make that penny disappear,' you say. 'Hold tight to my wrist and try to stop the penny flying away. But you won't be able to stop it because the magic is too strong. Ready? Penny, fly!'

You open your hand and everyone is astonished to see that the penny has vanished.

How to do it

Conjurers as a rule do not tell their audience what they are going to do, because if they did it might help the audience to spot how they did it. But in this trick you can safely say you are going to make the penny vanish from your hand because, what do you think? You don't put the penny into your hand in the first place.

When you put your hand into your pocket for the penny you simply say, 'For this piece of magic I need a penny.'

You take out several coins, and among them of course you must have a penny. 'I think I have a penny here somewhere,' you say. 'Yes, here it is.' You get hold of the penny between your finger and thumb and show it. Then you say, 'We don't want the other coins.' You put your hand back in your pocket and apparently leave the other coins behind, bringing your hand out again holding just the penny. That is what you lead the audience to believe. But what you really do is to leave all the coins, including the penny, in your pocket. You bring out your empty hand, with finger and thumb held together as if the penny were still there, and immediately put the finger and thumb into your left hand. Close the left hand and take the empty right hand away.

Up to now you haven't told the audience what you are going to do with the penny so they will take it for granted that the penny is in your left hand. Now you can get someone to hold your wrist and do anything else they like to stop the penny flying away. But of course as the penny isn't really there, you can easily make it vanish, just by opening your hand.

GROUP
MAGIC

People play games in groups, they learn lessons in groups and they even eat meals in groups. So why shouldn't they do magic in groups?

Of course in stage shows, they do. You have a high-powered illusionist sawing ladies in two and making motor cars disappear, assisted by no end of dashing dames and genteel gentlemen. And off stage, where the audience can't get at them, are other people frantically turning the lights up and down, hauling curtains, stuffing rabbits into boxes and goodness knows what.

Then in secret workshops there are absolutely hordes of mechanic sort of men and painter sort of people and carpenter sort of chaps, not to mention sewing sort of sisters, all busy making the things the magician does his magic with.

Now I think it would be a daisy of an idea if the intrepid readers of this book got themselves into groups with the same kind of purpose. You can get a few friends together and perhaps with the help of a friendly teacher or scoutmaster or cub mistress you could form a pretty nifty magic group.

One member of the group could do the actual magic, two or possibly three could act as assistants on the stage, bringing things on and taking them off and holding them and so on. Somebody else could be stage manager and see that everyone took the right thing on at the right time. Another grouper could work the music, putting records on. In fact you might go so far as to scoop in the school's percussion band if there is one, to play for the show. Or some of the group could make the music by playing the piano or the accordion or the double-acting steam trombone, or whatever musical engine they can almost play.

The ladies of the group could be mighty useful doing all that sewing you need for making trick handkerchiefs and things. Those who fancy themselves at fancy carpentry or cardboard work, or in fact any of the arts and crafts they're supposed to learn at school, could put their learning to practical use, helping to make the magic things needed for the show.

In this way you could work up a very effective show to be let off at church bazaars, school concerts, parish beanfeasts and other exotic occasions. You could sometimes help to earn money for deserving causes. And it wouldn't be altogether unreasonable if you sometimes earned a weeny bit of lolly for spending on making the show better.

Doing magic this way you will naturally have to rehearse the whole thing in the proper professional way. But that's a very good thing. Conjurers, even slightly professional conjurers, are sometimes inclined to dodge this rehearsing business and then things are apt to get a bit muddled up during the performance. And Puffins can't have that, can they? No answer required.

Magic done in groups can be a great deal of fun. Not only in the actual performing but in making the things you need for the show. In fact you'll probably find that getting together and making these things will give you just as much pleasure as doing the performing. Makes a nice change from playing ferocious pop records and driving Mum round the bend in other ways.

Now and again the members of the group can change jobs around if they like. Somebody else can do the performing while the used-to-be performer acts as assistant. Stage assistants can take a turn working the curtains or doing some other off-stage job.

Even if you do only little shows at home and for friends

you can still have a group of you working together. Sometimes you can do a show in which two or three people take it in turns to do tricks, rather in the way the old time concert parties used to take it in turns to sing select songs and recite polite recitations.

Naturally this group magic business doesn't prevent you from performing on your own. In fact you might use the group idea in another way. You could have two or three skinny groups of two or three people each. These little groups could then do little shows in competition with one another, something like an Eisteddfod only different. The magic societies often give entertainments of this kind, in which different performers do their own acts and prizes are given for the best.

In whatever way you do your magic shows, whether by yourself or in groups, always plan your programme of tricks the right way. It's no good going on and letting off a whole lot of assorted magic without considering in what order the tricks should be done.

A good general plan is this. Start the show with a fairly quick trick and, if possible, one that ends with a surprise. That gets the attention of the audience right away and lets them know that you're worth looking at, which of course you will be after studying this book.

Follow this with a trick that has plenty of mystery to it. The kind of magic that will make people scratch their heads and wonder how on earth it could be done. 'Broken Biscuits', which I have described in this book, is a good example of the sort of thing I mean.

Now carry on with a variety of tricks, doing a short trick between two that take a long time. If you are going to do several tricks with the same objects, for instance several card tricks or several tricks with a handkerchief, do them all together in a little group, don't space them out so that you have to keep coming back to do a trick with something you did a trick with several items before.

Then finish up with as showy a trick as you can manage. The grand finale trick needn't be a world-shaking mystery. As long as you produce a nice showy display to finish up with, you'll get the applause all right.

Whether you're giving a little show all by yourself, to a few friends, or letting off something rather more elaborate with a group of people, one thing you must have, behind the scenes, is what performers call a cue sheet. This is a fair size sheet of paper or cardboard on which you print in nice bold letters the tricks you are going to do, in the order you are going to do them. And under each trick you print the things that have to be brought on during the show. If you are using an assistant you can put on the cue sheet any special things the assistant has to do, at the places where he has to do them. If you have two assistants, working from different sides of your stage, have a cue sheet on each side with the necessary reminders on each.

This cue sheet will save you an awful lot of scarey worryings. You, or your assistants, take a look at this sheet every time you or they go behind the scenes. It will remind you, or them, what to do next. Of course you will have memorized this, but in the excitement of a performance you can forget things, and the cue sheet reminds you. It's one of the big secrets of giving a smoothly running performance.

And now good luck with your Puffin Magic and let's hope nobody throws anything but bouquets.